The Spirit in the Church

p. 29 - charismata > gord
30
41
42 - Church's Teaching
44   "   " "Mystici Corporis"
46   Scripture Ref.
47 - Imp. - "Gifts"
49 - Imp. -
50   "
51 + 52 priests/rel.

56
58 + 59 - other charismata
60 - Off. above making
62 - use democracy
64 - charismatic element preserved
65 - Unity/diversity of gifts
66 - Charisma/Suffering
68-69- vs. competition
          courage to "stay in there"
72-73
77 Criteria for Visions
81-82 Prophecies / Criteria
      83
mclusin *   84 - "movements from God!
      85-86

Imp * 89 - Prophecies
      94
      96 - Prophet

*   98 Theology of
            Prophecy
      103 True Prophecies
*   103 Scripture
      104
Imp 104
      Good Conclusion!

Karl Rahner

The Spirit in the Church

A CROSSROAD BOOK
THE SEABURY PRESS · NEW YORK

Second printing
1979
The Seabury Press
815 Second Avenue, New York, N.Y. 10017

Translated from the original German *Erfahrung des Geistes* published by
Verlag Herder of Freiburg im Breisgau, Federal Republic of Germany, in
1977, and copyright © Verlag Herder Freiburg im Breisgau 1977; from
Das Dynamische in der Kirche published by Verlag Herder in 1962 and
copyright © Herder KG 1962; and from *Visionen und Prophezeiungen*
published by Verlag Herder in 1962 and copyright © Herder KG 1962.
   The translation of *Erfahrung des Geistes* by John Griffiths is published
here for the first time and is copyright © Search Press Limited 1979; the
translation of 'Das Charismatische in der Kirche' from *Das Dynamische
in der Kirche* by W.J. O'Hara was first published in the Federal Republic
of Germany and in London by Herder and Burns & Oates in 1964; it
appears here in a revised version and is copyright © Herder KG 1964,
1978. The translation of two sections from *Visionen und Prophezeiungen*
was made by Charles Henkey and Richard Strachan and was first published in the Federal Republic of Germany and in London by Herder and
Burns & Oates in 1963; it appears here in a revised version and is
copyright © Herder KG 1963, 1978.

Printed in the United States of America

Library of Congress Cataloging in Publication Data

Rahner, Karl, 1904-
The spirit in the church.
Translation of Erfahrung des Geistes.
"A Crossroad book."
1. Holy Spirit. 2. Gifts, Spiritual. I. Title.
BT121.2.R33313   234'.1   79-1794   ISBN 0-8164-2189-7

Contents

PART I
Experiencing the Spirit

At Pentecost the Spirit was given to the young Church with the promise that he would always remain with the Church, until the end, in all his freedom, comfort and power. Therefore any meditation on the Holy Spirit must think of him as the gift in which God bestows himself on man.

The testimony of Scripture and the experience of the Spirit

Can we say anything more precise about the Spirit? We could of course turn to the Bible and search through it for all the passages in which we read of the Spirit of the Father given through the Son to all who believe in him; of the Spirit pouring as living water from the pierced side of the crucified Jesus, a source of vitality springing into everlasting life and assuaging our thirst for eternity; of the Spirit who makes us sons and allows us to say: Abba — dear Father; of the Spirit given to us in baptism and the laying on of hands. That is the Spirit who signifies the advent of the triune God and offers us a share in God's love, truth and freedom; in whom we all become one and in whom we all hope together; through whom we are anointed and sealed; and who with his inconceivable summoning power prays in us and with us, and in access to the Father gives us the assurance of a life that will last for ever. The Bible tells us all that and much more that is marvellous, impressive and exalted, offering many possibilities for meditation on the Spirit, so that we are

3

stirred to strong and courageous faith and true joy.

A believing Christian who opens his heart to this encouragement and consolation of the Bible will soon realize that he can also meditate thus today on the pentecostal mystery. It is also clear, but has to be made emphatically clear, that when we attempt to follow a somewhat different way of meditating and inquire into our own experience of the Spirit, we must still have implicit recourse to this same scriptural teaching. We would not be able so precisely to contemplate and understand our own experience (that available to all men in the profundity of their existence) if the Bible had not already expressly raised it to the level of personal concern.

But Scripture speaks in other than doctrinal terms of the Spirit who is given to us.

The Bible refers to our own experience of the Spirit (for instance, in Galatians and on other occasions in Paul, in John, and throughout Scripture), and therefore we are especially entitled to ask where and how we experience the Spirit in our own selves in this personal, biblical way.

Individual experiences and the one fundamental experience of the individual

When we make this inquiry, we are of course aware from the start that experience of this kind is incommensurable with what we are otherwise accustomed to call 'experience' in everyday life; especially in the sense given to the word by the physical sciences or empirical psychology. This experience of the Spirit begins at the innermost core of our existence, at its subjective pole, so to speak. It does not mean an encounter with any kind of object that confronts us from without, or the effects of such an occurrence. Apart from experiences which may be given an expressly theological interpretation in

4

our conscious mind and in our reflection on them, there is an experience within us which is of a different nature and irreconcilable with the experiences which first come to mind when we hear the word 'experience'.

When we first consider the associations of the word, we might think of the givenness, the occurrence as we notice it, of individual aspects of the reality of our human and objective environment, or of individual psychological phenomena within our conscious minds, as with a localized pain, or individual thoughts with a specific content, and so on. All these individual realities become present to us one by one, as it were, *within* the overall framework of our consciousness, where they are ranked, distinguished from others and connected to or associated with one another.

But in addition to these individual experiences of specific realities, there is another kind of experience which is outside the context of our everyday experiences as we recognize and talk about them. This is the experience of the individual person as such, who undergoes all those particular experiences as his own and is responsible for them; and who is present to himself in his original unity and oneness, even when he cannot see himself clearly and precisely in the details of his experience, but possesses himself only in an apparently empty disposition, and when he loses himself in the multitude of everyday experiences and seems to forget that wholeness.

My intention here is not to write a metaphysical or ontological essay on the isolated cognitive or existential nature of the fundamental experience which the individual human being has of himself: a unique, original basic experience which always remains hidden behind all the specific objective experiences of that same being (though I shall return later in an appropriate context to this 'transcendental' subjective nature of the human individual). At this point all I want to do is to remind you that there is a form of experience which is incommensurable with ordinary everyday encounters with specific realities, but which is no less present at all times, though in most cases we tend to ignore it. Similarly, the experience of the Spirit with which I am particularly concerned here is not to be rejected out of hand as non-existent, merely because — like the self-givenness of the human individual — it is liable to be overlooked in all specific experience.

Of course it is possible, when one thinks one cannot properly discover this experience of the Spirit in oneself, to assert its existence so to speak authoritatively from without in terms of Scripture and church doctrine. But if we did not inquire here and now into that experience of the Spirit — however important it might be to interpret it through faith and with the aid of holy writ and thus to bring it to the light of the word — then we should run into the danger of treating everything that Scripture says about that Spirit in us as ideology or mythology, and of asking almost petulantly whether, and where exactly, all the joyous possession of the Spirit we read about in the Bible is to be found in us. There is the further danger of asking (while still accepting the authority of Scripture) whether it should not all be transferred to a dimension somewhere outside our own consciousness and our freely-chosen piety.

Is there such a thing as experiencing the Spirit?

Is there such a thing as experience of the Spirit which on the one hand enables us to understand and legitimate the testimony of Scripture to the indwelling of the Spirit in us, and on the other hand is confirmed and affirmed by Scripture as the true Word? Indeed there is.

That assertion is not contradicted by the fact that we can and must ask in an inquiring and even doubting spirit about the possibility of such an experience; that it is not a question of an unquestioning experience, such as we have of the external world, without (apart from the belief of philosophers of the sublime) any need or necessity to feel or ask whether there really is such an experience of the human and material environment of man. There are other genuine experiences which are given and which we nevertheless have to inquire into and about beforehand. If, for example, a German idealist philosopher or a modern Christian philosopher inquires into the transcendental subject of knowledge and freedom, and asks about its structures, and if a modern depth psychologist tries to dredge up ultimate repressions and hidden attitudes, in both cases it is right to say that a human being can exhibit real experiences which are made in an unthematic way, are not verbalized and are perhaps repressed and not accepted by the free attention of a human being. Experience and objectified, material and verbalized experience are not simply one and the same thing, as the human consciousness lost and involved in the objectivity of everyday happenings might think. It is possible to have a kind of experience which is also an authentic quest and question.

The quest for the experience of the Spirit cannot be rejected from the start as contradictory. But how are we to go about it?

The testimony of the mystics

Today as so often in the Church's past it is probably appropriate to our quest to remember that there have always been mystics and enthusiastic or 'charismatic' experiences and movements in the Church which, in spite of their extremely diverse forms and interpretations, have been taken as experience of the Holy Spirit.

Mysticism has existed and still exists. Those graced with such

7

an experience have reported and continue to report that (either in a sudden breakthrough or in an extended series) they experience grace, the direct presence of God, and union with him in the Spirit, in the sacred night, or in a blessed illumination, in a void silently filled by God. They say that, at least within the mystical occurrence itself, they do not doubt that they experience the direct presence of the self-communicating God as the action and actuality of God's saving grace in the depths of their existence, and that that experience is the 'experience of the Holy Spirit'.

But the ordinary and theological ways in which this experience has been described are most various in the history of mysticism, and this objective and verbal inter-pretation (dependent on ideological, cultural and philosophical and theological modes and patterns of under-standing) has been offered in very different ways.

How the question is to be answered in accordance with the elation of this Christian mysticism and its Christian interpretation of similar non-Christian mystical phenomena, especially in the East and above all in Islam and in Buddhism, and how such experience can co-exist with socio-ecclesial and sacramental-ritual piety — are questions which do not concern us here and now.

The mystics bear witness to experience of the Spirit, and in principle there is nothing to stop us accepting all their testimonies as credible. That is the case especially when we remember that the original experience and the philosophical and theological interpretation of it are two different things, and that for that reason variety and contradiction in explanations do not discredit the original experience. On the other hand, these mystics included men of extreme sobriety and the finest observation, right up to Carl Albrecht in our own era — a mystic who was also a prominent doctor, psychologist, philosopher and scientist. There certainly are people who have the courage to offer credible testimony of their experience of the Spirit.

Of course theologians of Christian mysticism have stressed the extraordinary, reserved nature of these mystical phenomena. They have done so on the one hand because they wanted (quite rightly) to emphasize the origin of these phenomena in grace, and were guided by the implicit opinion that the work of grace and that which was free from all guilt must by definition occur but seldom; and on the other hand because such unmistakable mystical phenomena usually occur with accompanying ecstatic (indeed almost parapsychological) circumstances, which can of course be very rare. It is to some extent understandable that a normal Christian should treat such mystical occurrences as something that does not concern him and that he can safely ignore.

But if we isolated the mystical core-experience more exactly from such unusual peripheral phenomena as ecstasy, trance and so on (something not possible in the present context), then it would certainly be easier to see that such mystical experiences are not events that are sadly beyond the experience of an ordinary Christian, but that the testimony that mystics offer of their experiences indicates an experience which every Christian (and in fact every human being) can make and evoke but which he or she too easily overlooks or represses. In any case it is true to say that there is such a thing as mysticism, and that it is not so very distant from us as at first we are inclined to think.

Longing for the power of the Spirit

Enthusiastic phenomena and movements occur among non-Catholic as well as Catholic Christians. Whether such incidents represent mystical closeness to and oneness with God in the sense of the classical, more individual and individualist

9

mysticism, and how we can phenomenologically and theologically classify mysticism and (earlier and present-day) enthusiasm of a more communual type, is a question which I cannot examine closely here, especially since the traditional theology of mysticism recognizes the most diverse modes and stages of mystical experience, and hence there is a possibility of arranging enthuiastical or 'charismatic' experiences in a mystical hierarchy of some kind, without confusing them with the apex of mysticism: ultimate union with God in grace in the *unio mystica* itself.

Nevertheless there are Christian enthusiastic or charismatic movements nowadays. Their members are looking for the experience and power of the Spirit. They hold long charismatically-inspired prayer meetings at which they claim to experience the workings of the Spirit even in the form of ecstatic glossolalia (or speaking in tongues), and miraculous healing. A surprising number of people believe that in such prayer meetings they experience what they think of as baptism in the Spirit: an ultimate fulness of the Spirit.

Even an objective and rational theology does not have to reject all these enthusiastic experiences out of hand, or to treat them with doubt and scepticism; that is so even when it is evident that divine fire is producing an awful lot of human smoke, when a number of American charismatic efforts do not suit European taste, when a lot of these happenings can easily be explained by a very secular psychology, and when they occur just as often outside the religious context (though there they are not subjected to any theological interpretation).

Even though a man or woman who is still following his or her pilgrim way in time and history cannot really claim that he or she is fulfilled in such charismatic movements, having received an absolutely certain and ultimate message from the Spirit (traditional theology would call this confirmation or establishment in grace and count it among the most sublime of mystical experiences), here we are certainly confronted with especially impressive, humanly affective, liberating experiences of grace which offer wholly novel existential horizons. These mould the innermost attitude of a Christian for a long time, and are quite fit (if you wish) to be called 'baptism in the Spirit'. They are experienced in these charismatic services as the operation of the Spirit given to the community.

Can we experience the Spirit?

But — and here we reach the theme proper — what if we do not dare to call ourselves mystics, and perhaps for very different reasons cannot take any personal part in these charismatic movements and practices? Do we have any experience of the Spirit? Do we merely nod respectfully in the direction of other people's experiences which we ourselves find rather élitist? Do such people merely offer reports of a country that we have never seen and whose existence we are content to accept much as we might credit that of Australia if we have never been there?

We accept, and even confess as Christians supported by the testimony of Scripture, that we can have such an experience of the Spirit, and *must* have it as something offered to us in our essential freedom. That experience *is* given to us, even though we usually overlook it in the pursuit of our everyday lives, and perhaps repress it and do not take it seriously enough.

Experiencing the unutterable mystery

If I try to bring the reader's attention to such experiences, it seems inevitable that a few theoretical remarks on the innermost nature of human knowledge and freedom should precede more practical statements about personal experience.

11

The reader will have to excuse the summary and rather abstract nature of what I have to say in a somewhat restricted space. Only by talking about knowledge and freedom can I show and analyze the structure and specific nature of our spiritual experiences, and indicate why in our reflective, verbalizing objective minds we can easily overlook those experiences, and imagine that they do not exist at all. Therefore I request special patience and attention in considering my initial theological remarks.

We should consider human knowledge and freedom together, because in spite of the great differences between them, ultimately they have a common structure. In knowledge and freedom man becomes the very essence of transcendence. That may sound rather pretentious but it is unavoidable, and what I refer to in these terms is, in the end, the ultimate ineradicable essential structure of man, irrespective of whether the everyday man and the empirical scientist care to notice it or not. In knowledge and freedom man is always simultaneously concerned with the individually characterized and specifically definable individual object of his everyday experience and his individual sciences, *and* at the same time with something beyond all that — even when he takes no notice and does not name or refer to this 'something else' always present outside and beyond the ordinary. The movement of the mind or spirit towards the individual object with which he is concerned always aims at the particular object *by* passing beyond it. The individually and specifically and objectively known thing is always grasped in a broader, unnamed, implicitly present horizon of possible knowledge and possible freedom, even if the reflective mind only with difficulty and only subsequently succeeds in making this implicitly present fragment or aspect of consciousness a really specific object of consciousness, and thus objectively verbalizes it.

12

The movement of the spirit and of freedom, and the horizon of this movement, are boundless. Every object of our conscious mind which we encounter in our social world and environment, as it announces itself as it were of itself, is merely a stage, a constantly new starting-point in this movement which continues into the everlasting and unnamed 'before-us'. Whatever is given in our everyday and scientific consciousness is only a minute isle (though it may be big in one sense and may be magnified by our objectifying knowledge and action, and continuously and increasingly so) in a boundless ocean of nameless mystery, that grows and becomes all the clearer the more, and the more precisely, we express our knowing and wanting in the individual and specific instance. If we tried to set a boundary to this empty-seeming horizon of our consciousness, we would find that we had already passed through and beyond that very barrier that we sought to establish.

In the midst of our everyday awareness we are blessed or damned (have it how we will) in regard to that nameless, illimitable eternity. The concepts and words which we use subsequently to talk of this everlastingness to and into which we are constantly referred, are not the original actual mode of being of that experience of nameless mystery that surrounds the island of our everyday awareness, but merely the tiny signs and idols which we erect and have to erect so that they constantly remind us of the original, unthematic, silently offered and proffered, and graciously silent experience of the strangeness of the mystery in which, in spite of all the light offered by the everyday awareness of things, we reside, as if in a dark night and a pathless wilderness. (There we are in darkness and a desert place — but one that reminds us of the abyss in whose depths we are grounded but can never plumb).

Anyone who wants to can, of course, irritably and as if

tried too far, let the matter drop and continually repress it. He can try to ignore the night that alone makes our tiny lights visible and enables them to shine forth. But then a man acts against his own ultimate being, because this experience of his orientation to boundless mystery, if seen for what it really is, is not some extraneous spiritual luxury but *the* condition for the very possibility of everyday knowing and wanting (even though he usually overlooks this and fails to consider it in the to-and-fro of everyday life and the pursuit of knowledge).

If we were to use the term 'mysticism' to describe this experience of transcendence in which we always, even in the midst of everyday life, extend beyond ourselves and the specific thing with which we are concerned, we might say that mysticism occurs in the midst of everyday life, but is hidden and undeclared, and that this is the condition of the very possibility of even the most ordinary, sober and secular everyday experience.

God, the inclusive but illimitable ground

In this unnamed and unsignposted expanse of our consciousness there dwells that which we call God. The mystery pure and simple that we call God is not a special, particularly unusual piece of objective reality, something to be added to and included in the other realities of our naming and classifying experience. He is the comprehensive though never comprehended ground and presupposition of our experience and of the objects of that experience. He is experienced in this strange experience of transcendence, even though it may not be possible to arrive at a more exact metaphysical characterization of the unity and variety between the transcendental experience of the spiritual subject in knowledge and freedom, on the one hand, and the experience of God himself which is given in the transcendental experience, on the other hand. This kind of definition is too difficult a philosophical undertaking and unnecessary in the present context.

Nevertheless, the unlimited extent of our spirit in knowledge and freedom, which is ineluctably and unthematically given in every ordinary experience, allows us to experience what is meant by God as the revealing and fulfilling ground of that expanse of the Spirit and its unlimited movement. Transcendental experience, even when and where it is mediated through an actual categorial object, is always divine experience in the midst of everyday life.

The unrestricted movement of the Spirit and the bestowal of grace

At this point I must add a statement that is both philosophical and theological in a special, reciprocally conditional way. The boundless transcendental movement of the human spirit to God is so radical that this movement does not merely take God as an asymptotic goal that is always at an infinite distance, but as that which itself directly comprises the attainable goal of that movement.

Philosophically speaking, we can conceive and hope in this radical aspect by which God in himself becomes the goal of this movement, at least as a possibility that cannot be excluded. Theologically speaking, we do grasp this possibility as actually given by God; we use the term 'grace' for the actually given radical aspect of the transcendental movement to the immediacy of God in himself, right up to future direct perception. This comprises the actual and ultimate essence and nature of what we call grace, the self-communication of God in the Holy Spirit, and of what has its ultimate fulfilment in the direct loving contemplation of God. Existentially

15

speaking, we freely conceive this radical nature of our movement towards God which is supported by the Spirit of God, when we entrust ourselves unreservedly and unconditionally to the movement of the Spirit; as far in fact as it can actually go when in our freedom we set it no bounds but, so to speak, allow it to move right out, in its own boundlessness, and up to the immediacy of God himself.

If grace is understood thus, if it is understood philosophically as possibility, seen theologically as reality and realized existentially in hope (thematically or unthematically), then in the factitious order of reality, transcendental experience which is experience of God is always experience of grace, because the radicality of the experience of transcendence and its dynamic thrust is borne by the self-communication of God which makes all this possible in the innermost midst of our existence. It is borne by God's self-communication as the goal and power of a movement towards him which we call grace or the Holy Spirit (at least as an offer made to human freedom). Transcendental experience that allows God to be present is always (on account of the salvific will of God in regard to all men, by reason of which man is directed to the immediacy of God) experience of the Holy Spirit, irrespective of whether a man can or cannot reflectively interpret in this way his ineradicable experience of the nameless God, and whether theological terms of the kind we have used are available to him.

I must add something to the foregoing: everything that has been said is also true of the average everyday experience of man in knowledge and freedom, but it is always true of circumstances in which spiritual knowledge and freedom are given, in which a man exists as a real subject and enjoys his reference to ultimate validity by way of and beyond himself. This transcendental experience of God in the Holy Spirit is however given only unthematically in everyday

16

human experience, where it is overlaid and hidden by concern with actual realities with which we are taken up in our social world and environment. This transcendental experience of God in the Holy Spirit in everyday life remains anonymous, unreflective, and unthematic, like the generally and diffusely extended light of a sun that we do not see as such, turning instead to the individual objects of our sensuous experience as they become visible in the light.

Everyday experience and the experience of the Spirit

But even if we ignore the question whether such transcendental experience of God in the Holy Spirit could properly occur in instances of undirected absorption, in a state of consciousness void of objects of any specific kind, and in mystical experience for its own sake, there are in any case actual experiences in our existential history in which this intrinsically given transcendental experience of the Spirit occurs more obviously in our conscious minds: experiences in which (to put it the other way round) the individual objects of knowledge and of freedom with which we are concerned in everyday life, by their very specificity more clearly and insistently reveal the accompanying transcendental spiritual experience, in which by themselves and implicitly they indicate that inconceivable mystery of our existence that always surrounds us and also supports our everyday awareness, and indicate it more clearly than is otherwise usual in our ordinary and banal everyday life. Then everyday reality of itself refers to this transcendental experience of the Spirit which is implicitly and apparently featurelessly there and always there.

This indication, which is always associated with our everyday reality conceived in knowledge and freedom, and more insistently brought to our attention in certain situations, can also be intrinsically given by reason of the positive nature of that categorical reality in which the magnitude and glory, goodness, beauty and illumination of our individual experiential reality promise and point to eternal light and everlasting life. But it is already understandable that such a form of reference is most clearly experienced where the graspable contours of our everyday realities break and dissolve; where failures of such realities are experienced; when lights which illuminate the tiny islands of our everyday life go out, and the question becomes inescapable whether the night surrounding us is the absurd void of death engulfing us, or the blessed holy night which is already illumined from within and gives promise of everlasting day. When therefore I refer in the following primarily to those experiences which in this second way allow transcendental experience of God in the Holy Spirit to go forward, that does not mean that people and Christians are forbidden to let this experience of God occur in the first way, and thus to receive it. Ultimately the *via eminentiae* and the *via negationis* are not two ways or two stations one behind the other on a way, but two aspects of one and the same experience (though, as I have remarked, for the sake of clarity it is quite justifiable to lay special stress on the *via negationis*).

Experiencing the Spirit in actual life

I can now refer to the actual life-experiences which, whether we come to know them reflectively or not, are experiences of the Spirit. It is important that we experience them in the right way. In the case of these indications of the actual experience of the Spirit in the midst of banal everyday life, it can no longer be a question of analyzing them individually right down to their ultimate depth — which is the Spirit. And no attempt can be made to make a systematic tabular summary of such experiences. Only arbitrarily and unsystematically selected examples are possible.

Let us take, for instance, someone who is dissatisfied with his life, who cannot make the good will, errors, guilt and fatalities of his life fit together, even when, as often seems impossible, he adds remorse to this accounting. He cannot see how he is to include God as an entry in the accounting, as one that makes the debit and credit, the notional and actual values, come out right. This man surrenders himself to God or — both more imprecisely and more precisely — to the hope of an incalculable ultimate reconciliation of his existence in which he whom we call God dwells; he releases his unresolved and uncalculated existence, he lets go in trust and hope and does not know how this miracle occurs that he cannot himself enjoy and possess as his own self-actuated possession.

There is a man who discovers that he can forgive though he receives no reward for it, and silent forgiveness from the other side is taken as self-evident.

There is one who tries to love God although no response of love seems to come from God's silent inconceivability, although no wave of emotive wonder any longer supports him, although he can no longer confuse himself and his life-force with God; although he thinks he will die from such a love, because it seems like death and absolute denial; because with such a love one appears to call into the void and the completely unheard-of; because this love seems like a ghastly leap into groundless space; because everything seems untenable and apparently meaningless.

There is one man who does his duty where it can apparently only be done, with the terrible feeling that he is denying himself and doing something ludicrous which no one will thank him for.

There is a man who is really good to another man from whom no echo of understanding and thankfulness is heard in return, whose goodness is not even repaid by the feeling of having been 'selfless', noble and so on.

There is one who is silent although he could defend himself, although he is unjustly treated, who keeps silence without feeling that his silence is his sovereign unimpeachability.

There is a man who obeys not because he must and would otherwise find it inconvenient to disobey, but purely on account of that mysterious, silent and inconceivable thing that we call God and the will of God.

There is a man who renounces something without thanks or recognition, and even without a feeling of inner satisfaction.

There is a man who is absolutely lonely, who finds all the right elements of life pale shadows; for whom all trustworthy handholds take him into the infinite distance, and who does not run away from this loneliness but treats it with ultimate hope.

There is a man who discovers that his most acute concepts and most intellectually-refined operations of the mind do not fit; that the unity of consciousness and that of which one is conscious in the destruction of all systems is now to be found only in pain; that he cannot resolve the immeasurable multitude of questions, and yet cannot keep to the clearly known content of individual experience and to the sciences.

There is one who suddenly notices how the tiny trickle of his life wanders through the wilderness of the banality of existence, apparently without aim and with the heartfelt fear of complete exhaustion. And yet he hopes, he knows not how, that this trickle will find the infinite expanse of the ocean, even though it may still be covered by the grey sands which seem to extend for ever before him.

One could go on like this for ever, perhaps even then without coming to that experience which for this or that man is the experience of the Spirit, freedom and grace in his life.

For every *one* man makes that experience in accordance with the particular historical and individual situation of his specific life. Every *one* man! But he has so to speak to dig it out from under the rubbish of everyday experience, and must not run away from it where it begins to become legible, as though it were only an undermining and disturbance of the self-evidence of his everyday life and his scientific assurance.

Let me repeat, though I must say it in almost the same words: where the one and entire hope is given beyond all individual hopes, which comprehends all impulses in silent promise,

— where a responsibility in freedom is still accepted and borne where it has no apparent offer of success and advantage,

— where a *person* man experiences and accepts his ultimate freedom which no earthly compulsions can take away from him,

— where the leap into the darkness of death is accepted as the beginning of everlasting promise,

— where the sum of all accounts of life, which no one can calculate alone, is understood by an inconceivable Other as good, though it still cannot be 'proven',

— where the fragmentary experience of love, beauty, and joy is experienced and accepted purely and simply as the promise of love, beauty and joy, without their being understood in ultimate cynical scepticism as a cheap form of consolation for some final deception,

— where the bitter, deceptive and vanishing everyday world is withstood until the accepted end, and accepted out of a force whose ultimate source is still unknown to us but can be tapped by us,

— where one dares to pray into a silent darkness and knows that one is heard, although no answer seems to come back about which one might argue and rationalize,

— where one lets oneself go unconditionally and

experiences this capitulation as true victory,

— where falling becomes true uprightness,

— where desperation is accepted and is still secretly accepted as trustworthy without cheap trust,

— where a man entrusts all this knowledge and all his questions to the silent and all-inclusive mystery which is loved more than all our individual knowledge which makes us such small people,

— where we rehearse our own deaths in everyday life, and try to live in such a way as we would like to die, peaceful and composed,

— where . . . (as I have said, we could go on and on):

 — there is God and his liberating grace. There we find what we Christians call the Holy Spirit of God. Then we experience something which is inescapable (even when suppressed) in life, and which is offered to our freedom with the question whether we want to accept it or whether we want to shut ourselves up in a hell of freedom by trying to barricade ourselves against it. There is the mysticism of everyday life, the discovery of God in all things; there is the sober intoxication of the Spirit, of which the Fathers and the liturgy speak which we cannot reject or despise, because it is real.

Living as people of the Spirit

Let us look for that experience in our own lives. Let us seek the specific experiences in which something like that happens to us. If we find them we have made the experience of the Spirit which we are talking about. The experience of eternity, the experience that the Spirit is more than a piece of this temporal world, the experience that the meaning of man is not contained purely in the meaning and happiness of this world, the experience of the wager and of the trust which

22

no longer possess any obvious ground taken from the success of this world.

From there, we can understand what kind of secret passion is alive in men of the Spirit and in the saints. They want to make this experience. They want repeatedly (out of a secret fear that they are caught up in the world) to ensure that they are beginning to live in the Spirit. They have tasted the Spirit. Whereas ordinary people treat such experience only as an unpleasant though not wholly avoidable disruption of normal life, in which the Spirit is only the seasoning and garnishing of another life but not of one's own, men of the Spirit and the saints have tasted pure Spirit. The Spirit is something they take pure and neat, as it were, no longer as a mere seasoning of earthly existence. Hence their remarkable life, their poverty, their longing for humility, their passionate wish for death, their readiness to suffer, their secret longing for martyrdom. It is not as if they were not also weak. It is not as if they did not also have continually to return to the ordinary atmosphere of everyday life. It is not as if they did not know that grace can also bless everyday life and rational action, and make them steps towards God. It is not as if they did not know that we are no angels in this life and are not expected to be. But they know that as a spirit man (in real existence and not merely in speculation) must really live on the borderline between God and the world, time and eternity, and they try continually to make sure that they are also really doing that, and that the Spirit in them is not only the means of a human way of life.

And if we make this experience of the Spirit, then (at least as Christians living in faith) we have already experienced the supernatural factually, even though very anonymously and perhaps inexpressibly. Probably so that we cannot veer round and should not veer round in order to see the supernatural itself. But we know if we release ourselves to this experience

23

of the Spirit, if the tangible, tellable and enjoyable founders, if everything sounds deathly silent, if everything has the taste of death and of downfall, or if everything disappears so to speak into an inconceivable, so to speak white, colourless and intangible blessedness, then not only the spirit but the Holy Spirit is actually at work in us. Then the hour of his grace has come. That is the time of the apparently strange groundlessness of our existence which we experience: the groundlessness of God who communicates himself to us, the beginning of the coming of his infinity, which no longer has any paths, which is enjoyed like nothingness because it is infinity. When we have cast off and no longer belong to ourselves, when we have denied ourselves and we have moved an infinite distance from ourselves, then we begin to live in the world of God himself, of the God of grace and eternal life.

That may seem unusual to us at first, and we are constantly tempted to take fright and return to the trustworthy and close at hand; indeed we often have to do so and should do so. Yet we should try to grow used to the taste of the pure wine of the Spirit, filled by the Holy Spirit. At least we should do so to an extent that enables us not to reject the chalice when it is proffered to us.

Everyday mysticism and the grace of Jesus Christ

At this point one might ask whether I have not hitherto praised a mysticism of everyday life which is not specifically Christian and directed to Jesus the crucified and risen Christ, but something which could be found in all religions, and even outside any expressly religious and theological interpretation. That is a question which I cannot answer adequately here, even though I can offer some indications on how it might be answered.

First: if and insofar as the experience of the Spirit I talk of here is also to be found in a mysticism of everyday life outside an verbalized and institutionalized Christianity, and therefore may be discovered by a Christian in his life when he encounters his non-Christian brothers and sisters, or in his study of religious history, a Christian need not be shocked or astonished at such a revelation. It should serve only to show that his God, the God of Jesus Christ, wants *all men* to be saved, and offers his grace as liberation to *all* men, offering it as liberation into inconceivable mystery. Then the grace of Christ takes effect in a mysterious way beyond the bounds of verbalized and institutionalized Christendom, and even outside those bounds allows people to share in the paschal mystery of Jesus, even where a man who is loyal to his conscience has not yet been reached in any convincing way by the explicit message of Christianity and has not been moulded by the Christian sacraments.

Such a revelation is not only something that is not forbidden to a Christian if and where he undergoes it. He should even expect it, because his faith requires him to believe in the universal saving will of God, which finds a barrier only in an individual's personal mortal guilt, and even offers every human being the grace of Christ again and again throughout his lifetime. The grace of God which has become victorious and irreversible in human history through the history of the one crucified and risen Man, is still the grace of Jesus Christ where it is not expressly and reflectively conceived and interpreted as such. That is not only something that a Christian should opine; it is an actual part of his faith if he believes in the universal and supernatural saving will of God for all men, and it forbids him to believe that that salvific will operates for a man's salvation only if he has already expressly embraced Christianity.

Sharing in the victorious death of Jesus

If we consider what I have already said about the human transcendental experience absolutized by the grace of God and allowed entry into the ineffable mystery of God, we see that it has something to do with the death of Jesus, irrespective of whether this is expressly conceived of or not.

Originally and ultimately, the actual and freely accepted experience of transcendence in the Holy Spirit is no matter of theoretical reason but one of the whole man in the actual history of his life and of his freedom. Therefore it occurs ultimately where it is impossible to stop at some particular reality in life and treat it as final and absolute; it occurs where an ultimate autonomous urge to self-defence is surrendered in free and liberated hope with no other protection; it occurs, in short, where one dies into the inconceivability of God.

 If a Christian, by reason of his relationship with the absolute God, cannot and will not leave his historical existence open, the moment of his mystical union with God and therefore the apex of his experience of the Spirit is ultimately given not so much in a sublime mystical experience of immersion or inward communion as such, as in his death. It occurs in death though not necessarily in the moment of his medical *exitus*. Conversely, moreover, his actual existential death in certain circumstances (though not necessarily) may occur as ultimate self-abandonment, which is death indeed, in a mystical experience of immersion which cannot occur before one is dead in the usual sense of the word. Experience of the Spirit and sharing in the victorious death of Jesus, only in which the true good fortune of our death is experienced in a community of faith, are one and the same thing. In this life the chalice of the Holy Spirit is identical with the chalice of Christ. But only that man drinks from it who has slowly learnt — to some extent — how to find fulness in emptiness, uprightness in downfall, life in death, and discovery in abandonment. Whoever learns these things undergoes the experience of the Spirit, of pure Spirit, and in this experience meets with the experience of the Holy Spirit of grace. For, on the whole, ultimately one reaches this liberation of the spirit only by the grace of Christ in faith. When He liberates the spirit, he liberates it through supernatural grace and then releases it into the life of God himself.

Before I close this part, I must make two points which refer back to the point at which I began, and to which I hope they have kept fairly close. I refer to the connexion between the experience of the Spirit and everyday life.

Experiencing the Spirit is not élitist

The experience of the Spirit I have described here has nothing to do with any élitist consciousness of being one of the elect who are set apart from the great majority of average Christians and human beings. If the foregoing is properly understood then experience of the Spirit as I have described it occurs constantly in the life of anyone who is alive to personal self-possession and to the action of freedom, and truly in control of his entire self. In most human lives that does not happen as meditation proper, in self-immersive inward communion, and so on, but in the warp and weft of every-day life, where responsibility, loyalty, love and so on are practised absolutely, and where ultimately it is a secondary question whether such behaviour is accompanied by any expressly religious interpretation. That does not mean, however, that any such thematically religious interpretation is not correct and important in itself. Meditation and similar spiritual 'exercises' are not to be devalued. They can be a

27

form of training for the occasion when ultimate experiences of the Spirit (wherever they occur in life) are ordained and accepted in radical, absolute freedom. Such exercises can also (though not exclusively) afford the opportunity to experience the Spirit more clearly and reflectively. They should be grasped in the ultimate fundamental freedom of the human being so that they become a decision comprising the whole of existence and taking it into salvation.

Christianity is not élitist. If we look at the New Testament, it offers details of various sublime experiences of the Spirit that can be summarized as 'mystical'. But all men who selflessly love their neighbour and experience God in that love are accorded ultimate salvation by God's jurisdiction, which is not capped by the highest ascent or deepest immersion of the mystic. Therefore the New Testament, even when it does not expressly consider the point, is of the opinion that this insurpassable salvation in the self-communicating Holy Spirit of God can occur where apparently nothing more is happening than the final bitter duty of everyday life and a solitary death. Such an ultimate experience of the Spirit can occur in the midst of everyday life in spite of all the élitist pride of the 'pneumatics'.

Of course when there is genuine concern for salvation, and when God is loved, when a man learns ever more clearly that he can never come to a finally valid stop on the road of self-liberation, and when he submits to the hard though happy demands of the Sermon on the Mount, he will never refuse to take at least those expressly meditative and spiritual paths revealed to him in the ultimately inaccessible history of his life.

Everyday mission

When we read the letters of Paul we eventually come upon his

28

teaching about charismata, or charisms. These are not merely identical with a possession of the Spirit and the experience of the Spirit of a man justified by faith. But they do have an inward connexion with that possession of the Spirit and its form of experience. They are seen by Paul as versatile, always variously distributed capacities which are never all given to one individual; they also comprise a commission to construct a Christian community. They may – like healing powers or speaking in tongues – be quite extraordinary and even spectacular in nature. But they can also be almost secular, everday capabilities, up to the point of good cash administration of a parish or community. In a sense we can overlook the importance of these charismata for the construction of the *community*. We may say that all abilities and possibilities of Christian action, inasmuch as it is ultimately empowered, supported and ensouled by the Holy Spirit of God, are charismata or gifts of the Spirit.

Though we must not forget that the many separated Christians have in different ways one and the same possession of the Spirit, charismata are primarily quite sober individual commissions, individual abilities and individual offers, which make up the everydayness of a man and his manysided life. Such possibilities always exceed what an individual man (given the limitations of his strength and time) can actually accomplish. He has to choose and discern. If he makes this choice duly (that is, in the Spirit and acting from the Spirit), then what is chosen may certainly be called 'charisma' or the 'will of God.'

How is such a choice made? The masters of the spiritual life have thought much about and experimented with the rules for the discernment of spirits, and have showed their conviction that the discovery of what is actually right here-and-now is not *only* a matter for rational consideration and theoretical moral theology. There is no room here to

29

recapitulate these teachings of the spiritual masters. But the fundamentals I have outlined should help me to say some thing very short and basic but important which unites the ultimate experience of the Spirit and the constantly new, ultimately 'charismatic' individual decisions which life says have to be made. Whenever such a choice of any specific thing is not merely rationally justified and does not merely accord with the principles of Christian morality, but also (something far from obvious) does not displace or darken an ultimate openness to specific experience of the Spirit in unlimited freedom, where a Christian experiences as given a final, non-arbitrary, rationally indissoluble yet factually given synthesis of original experience and the inclination to a specific object from his everyday freedom, then that Christian has found the will of God. Then he acts not only rationally and morally but charismatically. Of course a great deal of practice and spiritual experience are necessary in order to recognize accurately occasions when an inclination to a specific object proffered by everyday life does not displace this ultimate experience of the Spirit into an apparent void freed of God, but becomes the starting-point for that experience of the Spirit and offers a successful synthesis of the experience of the Spirit and everyday duties.

But the experience of such a synthesis, in which a man leaves everything for the unlimited mystery of God, in which his courageous decision 'fits' the actual reality of life and the 'world', is possible and comprises the whole Christian life. In such a life, with the dying Jesus, a man leaves everything in order to enter the exitless and unsignposted freedom of God, *and* at the same time lovingly accepts the individual everyday aspects of this world that are allotted him, in order to take them with him into that Spirit of God.

We must look for experience of the Spirit and for grace in the contemplation of our own lives. But not so that we can say, 'That's him. Now I know where the Spirit blows'. That is not how the Spirit is discerned. He cannot be found by laying triumphant claim to him as if he were our possession and property. We can seek him only by forgetting self. We can find him only in seeking God and surrendering self in generous outgoing love, and without returning to self. Moreover we must continually ask whether anything like that annihilating and enlivening experience of Spirit is at work in us, so that we know how far we still have to go, and how distant what we presume to call our 'spiritual' life still is from real experience of the Holy Spirit.

Grandis nobis restat via. Venite et gustate, quam suavis sit Dominus! There is still a long way to go. Come and see how full the Lord is of loving-kindness!

PART II
The charismatic element in the Church

It is said that the Church was founded at Pentecost. It can also be said that Jesus established the Church by giving authority to Peter and the apostles. We hear an echo in Pius XII's encyclical *Mystici Corporis* of the view that the Church came into existence on the cross as the second Eve and mother of all the living, sprung from the pierced side of the second Adam who died there. These statements need not contradict one another, for each graphically expresses a facet of a complex occurrence which, because it concerns a society, not a physical event, cannot be assigned a quite determinate movement and date. To the nature of the Church there belongs its structure as a hierarchically-organized society with a variety of offices and authorities, and also the Spirit animating it like a soul, as well as the manifestation of this gift of the Spirit, for the Church has to bear witness through history precisely as such a Spirit-endowed society. Consequently, mention is made of the cross, as the event in which in the blood of the Redemption the Holy Spirit is given to mankind, and of Pentecost, when it is made known tangibly and by testimony that this Spirit has truly come.

1. The Charisma of Office

The Spirit is promised and given to the ecclesiastical ministry. The promise that the Lord will remain in his Spirit with the Church all days until the end of the world applies to the official Church. For if that were not guaranteed by the power of the promise, the official hierarchy of the Church as such could revolt against God and against the truth and grace of Christ; it could fall away from God and lose his grace. In that case it would really only be like the Synagogue which, founded by God in the covenant, broke the covenant. The Church would not be the new and everlasting covenant, the Church of the last days against which the gates of death cannot prevail. At all events it would not be the visibly hierarchically-constituted Church of the apostles, with its mission and discipleship, its ministry and Scripture, its written word, its visible sacraments, the Church of the Word made flesh. It would still be possible, of course, to hold even then that there was a 'Church', in so far as there were, and always would be, men seized and possessed by the Spirit that blows where it wills, so that the Church would ever be springing up anew. But that would not be the one abiding historical entity founded on the apostles and their enduring mission, remaining always the locus and visible manifestation of grace, its sacrament. Consequently the Spirit must be assured to ecclesiastical office as such, and so it is that the apostles and their disciples following them in historical succession are told that the Lord will be with them all days until the end of the world. It is not that men and the office they hold and their law are not in themselves in a position to rebel against the Spirit of Christ and do disown that Spirit, nor as if the Church, consisting as it does of men and therefore of sinners, were incapable of becoming the synagogue of Antichrist. But because the grace of God is not only offered to mankind as a possibility, but is promised to the Church as a victorious grace more powerful than sin, it is certain from the outset from God's side and from him alone, that ecclesiastical office in what most properly belongs to it, in its essence, will not, though it could, be used by men as a weapon against God. To that extent, therefore, ecclesiastical office and ministry is charismatic in character, if we understand by charismatic, what is in contradistinction to what is purely institutional, administered by men, subject to calculation and expressible in laws and rules.

That ecclesiastical ministry does not rebel against God and his Spirit, that in the last resort it does not abuse its power and force against God, cannot be ultimately ensured by anything pertaining to this power itself as a juridical, tangible element. There is no question of lodging an appeal against an alleged abuse of this power with some other tangible court of appeal, nor of stirring up a revolution against this ministry by claiming that it has unmistakably and confessedly offended against the spirit and the letter of its foundation, so that in consequence it has lost its *raison d'être*. And yet, because there is no section in the official constitution of the Church to which one could appeal against official authority and so be freed from its jurisdiction; and because the ministry cannot exclude by merely human means the mortal danger of an abuse of ecclesiastical authority that would destroy that authority itself; and because the official Church must, for all that, be preserved by God's grace against fundamental abuse, there belongs to ecclesiastical ministry as such a charismatic element, transcending the institutional order. It is usually referred to among Catholics as the assistance of the Holy Spirit that is accorded to ecclesiastical office and those who hold it. It is important, however, to be clear in one's mind what is involved in this simple statement. It implied that this assistance cannot entirely be reduced to juridical terms. It is not to be identified with the divine wisdom of the Church's laws, though both as principles of jurisprudence and as precepts of morality they prevent many abuses. It cannot be adequately translated into those laws. For, of course, there is no judicature in the Church where an appeal might be lodged from men to men, and there is no right to revolution. The first would abolish a human and tangible supreme court of appeal in the Church altogether, while the second would be a denial of the Church as an enduring visible historical entity with genuine continuity.

This is clearly to be seen, for example, in the fact that the highest seat of jurisdiction in the Church, the pope, also possesses competence to determine what his competence is. If he invokes his highest and ultimate authority, it is not possible to oppose his decision with the claim that he has exceeded his powers, acted *ultra vires*, and that his judgment is not binding on that account. For it is not possible to verify that he has kept within the scope of his competence by applying a criterion to him, as though by judicial process, to test his conduct. When he invokes his ultimate authority in making a decision, this action is itself the only guarantee that he has remained within the limits of his competence. But that means that such an office held by a human being, if it is not to be an absolute tyranny, must itself rise into a sphere to which no judicial criteria can be applied. It must necessarily itself be charismatic. And that means it is only conceivable if there is always added to it in fact and in idea a power which is itself indefectible, the assistance of the Spirit of God himself, permanently promised to it, even though this is not something that can be administered or comprised in legal terms.

Here, therefore, is an office which in order to be what it is, passes into the charismatic sphere. Consequently we also have here a case where the charismatic feature has not simply the character of being merely sporadic, intermittent. 'Charismatic', 'irreducible to juridical terms', 'given only now and again', are not the same thing. For that very reason, however, the 'charismatic' retains its incalculable character. That is taken very much as a matter of course by a Catholic.

He can only conceive the right functioning of an office, even of the highest in the Church, as the office (if we may so express it for the sake of clarity), acting in accordance with its true structure. He can very easily think of the office as functioning rightly because God so arranges things that it does not act, that the individual holder of office dies, that some power or other, external to it, impels it unexpectedly to act in a way different from what it would otherwise have done. It is clear, then, that according to Catholic belief the guarantee of the unfailing rightness of official action lies not in an intrinsic feature of the office as a human, juridical, tangible entity, but in God's assistance alone, and this can make use of every conceivable means, not necessarily connected with the office itself. Of course, all this does not mean (and for our further reflections later it is important to stress the fact), that the office in each of its manifestations is markedly 'charismatic'.

The theology of the Church has worked out with ever-increasing clarity when, to what degree and with what varying certainty this charismatic assistance of the Holy Spirit is promised to the Church's ministry. That is not my subject here. Every Catholic Christian knows, for example, that the charisma of infallibility only belongs to papal teaching authority under very definite, clearly-determined conditions. Everyone knows that the Church in the exercise of its pastoral office, in its legislation, administration, adaptation to the requirements of the age, pastoral practice, in its activity in art, learning and the shaping of Christian life in practice, can exhibit faults, omissions, partially mistaken developments, signs of sclerosis and reactionary tendencies. But it would be incompatible with the invincibly Christian character and holiness of the Church and contrary to an ecclesiastical spirit to maintain that, though infallible in its teaching, it is not, in its normal life and activity, under the guidance and direction

39

of the Spirit promised to it; or if one wanted to hold with a sort of mental obstinacy (there are such people), that more or less everything is wrong that the Church has in actual practice done in the course of history, except its solemn dogmatic definition, — as though the life of the Church amounted to practically nothing but sin and falling away from the mind of Christ. Such people may imagine they have a heroic love for the Church, of the 'in spite of everything' sort. In fact, they consider themselves to possess a mind of superior discernment to that of the actual average everyday Church. They do not believe in the charismatic character that belongs to the Church's ministry even in the everyday world, even under the routine of what is laborious and unpretentious and commonplace.

All this is merely intended to make it clear that office and spiritual gifts in the Church cannot be conceived as two totally distinct elements which happen to be united more or less by chance in a person who is endowed with office and yet at the same time with charisma. Office itself and not merely the actual man who in fact holds office must be characterized by charismatic gifts if the Church with its hierarchical constitution is to remain to the end the Church of the abiding Spirit, which through God's grace alone is incapable of falling in its totality from the grace, truth and holiness of God and of so turning the visible representative manifestation of grace (for that is what the Church is) into a synagogue devoid of the Spirit.

2. The Non-institutional Charismata

a. The thesis

It would be just as false, however, if one were to suppose that the charismatic element in the Church were to be reserved to its official ministry. There are, in fact, earnest Catholics who are anxious to have a right mind about the Church and who hold the view, tacitly and in the background, but all the more operative and dangerous on that account, that the hierarchy is the only vehicle of the Spirit or the only portal through which the Spirit enters the Church. They imagine the Church as a sort of centralized state, and a totalitarian one at that. We must distinguish between what we may perhaps for our present purpose call an absolute claim made by the Church, valid within certain limits and strictly circumscribed, and a totalitarian conception of the Church. For the Catholic the Church is absolute in the sense that he knows that the Church is the enduring and imperishable home of his salvation, the ground of truth, the inexhaustible well-spring of grace, the representative of the visible presence of Christ's grace until the end. And all this refers to the hierarchical Church. Consequently, for anyone who has once accepted by faith this Church as the measure of his life, there is no point of vantage outside this Church from which he might oppose it, no court of appeal to which he might take a claim against it. If he struggles and argues with it, it is a struggle and a debate within the Church itself. He is speaking to the human members and ministers of this Church and appealing to guiding principles and a spirit which they recognize as their own and to which they concede they are themselves subject and willingly subject. For a Catholic every 'clash' with the Church is always an occurrence recognized by the Church itself as an expression of its own life and only to the extent that it is such a thing.

In that sense, therefore, the Church is an 'absolute' for a Catholic, simply because it is one with Christ, who for him is the Absolute made man, and because it declares itself to be one with Christ, Here again, it is part of this faith in the union of the Church with Christ that it does not transgress

41

the limits set to this unity (although there is a perpetual temptation to do so), in the spheres where as bride and handmaid it is distinct from its Lord and stands essentially apart from him. But this attribution of an absolute character does not involve a totalitarian view of the Church. Such a conception would be totalitarian if anyone were to think, explicitly or tacitly, that the Church is not liable to err in any of its actions, if it were supposed that all living impulses of the Church can and may only originate from its official ministers, that any initiative in the Church is only legitimate if it springs expressly or at least equivalently from above and only after it has been authorized, that all guidance of the Holy Spirit always and in every case affects ecclesiastical office, God directing his Church only through its hierarchy and that every stirring of life in the Church is the mere carrying out of an order or a wish 'from above'. Such a false totalitarian view inevitably equates office and charisma, if any importance is left to this latter. But this is just what is not the case. For there are charismata, that is, the impulsion and guidance of God's Spirit for the Church, in addition to and outside its official ministry.

Now this thesis is not a private opinion but a doctrine taught by the Church's own magisterium, a doctrine of Scripture itself, and a truth lived and practised in the Church in every age, though this does not prevent its being more clearly and more explicitly realized by the Church's human members at certain times.

b. The Church's teaching

Pius XII wrote in the encyclical *Mystici corporis:* 'But it must not be supposed that this co-ordinated, or organic, structure of the Body of the Church is confined exclusively to the grades of the hierarchy, or — as a contrary opinion holds — that it consists only of "charismatics", or persons endowed with miraculous powers; though these, be it said, will never be lacking in the Church . . . But when the Fathers of the Church mention the ministries of this Body, its grades, professions, states, orders and offices, they rightly have in mind not only persons in sacred orders, but also all those who have embraced the evangelical counsels and lead either an active life among men, or a hidden life in the cloister, or else contrive to combine the two, according to the institution to which they belong, also those who, though living in the world, actively devote themselves to spiritual or corporal works of mercy; and also those who are joined in chaste wedlock. Indeed, it is to be observed, especially in present circumstances, that fathers and mothers and godparents, and particularly those among the laity who co-operate with the ecclesiastical hierarchy in spreading the kingdom of the divine Redeemer, hold an honoured place in the Christian society, and that they too are able, with the inspiration and help of God, to attain the highest degree of sanctity, which, as Jesus Christ has promised, will never be wanting in the Church . . .' Christ 'established that authority, determined by appropriate precepts, rights and duties, as the primary law of the whole Church. But our divine Saviour himself also governs directly the society which he founded; for he reigns in the minds and hearts of men, bending and constraining even rebellious wills to his decree. . . . And by this interior government he, "the shepherd and bishop of our souls", not only cares for each individual but watches over the whole Church: enlightening and fortifyiing its rulers so that they may faithfully and fruitfully discharge their functions, and (especially in circumstances of greater difficulty) raising up in the bosom of Mother Church men and women of outstanding sanctity to give example to other Christians and so promote the increase of his mystical Body." (*A.A.S.* XXXV [1943],

200ff.; *The Mystical Body of Jesus Christ* [London, 1948], pp. 13-14, 23-24).

If we reflect attentively on this teaching, it is possible for us to say that there are persons in the Church endowed with the charismatic gifts of the Spirit outside the sacred ministry. They are not merely recipients of orders from the hierarchy; they may be the persons through whom Christ 'directly' guides his Church. Obviously office is not thereby abolished. The Lord, of course, guides and rules his Church, the same encyclical tells us, through the medium of the sacred ministry. Holders of office themselves can receive, in addition to the authority of their charge and its proper administration under the protection of the Spirit, direct impulsions of that kind from the Church's Lord. But if Christ directly operates in his Church apart from the hierarchy, if he rules and guides the Church through charismata that are not linked to office and in this sense are extraordinary, and if, nevertheless, there is a valid and irrevocable official ministry in the Church, then harmony between the two 'structures' of the Church, the institutional and the charismatic, can only be guaranteed by the one Lord of both, and by him alone, that is to say, charismatically.

Now it is no doubt a rule, a normative principle and a law for the spiritual gifts themselves, that they should operate in an 'orderly' way, that they are not permitted to depart from the order prescribed by authority. As a consequence it is possible to use as a criterion of their authentic spiritual origin the fact whether or not they do this. Yet this formal rule alone would not of itself guarantee the actual existence of harmony. For though official authority might be sufficiently protected by the rule from merely apparent spiritual gifts, the charismata also need to be protected from the authorities. Provision has to be made that bureaucratic routine, turning means into ends in themselves, rule for the sake of rule and not for

44

the sake of service, the dead wood of tradition, proud and anxious barricades thrown up against new tasks and requirements, and other such dangers, do not extinguish the Spirit.

No really effective remedy against them is ensured by the formal principle that official authority must not extinguish the Spirit, any more than it is merely by the punishment that in the long run always falls on authority if it trusts more to the letter than to the Spirit. The effective guarantee is not given by official authority and its principles alone. Even though the authorities can only sin against the spiritual gifts by transgressing the very principles of their own authority, it is not thereby excluded that those in office might not discern their own principles clearly enough in the matter, that they might do prejudice to them and be in danger of excluding the charismatic element from the Church as a nuisance. A safeguard that is effective and certain to be effective is only to be looked for from the Lord of both. He is the transcendent source of both, and he himself is the support that he promised to his Church always and victoriously, consequently he can ensure the unity of the two elements. Their unity cannot itself be institutionally organized, it is itself charismatic, though this charisma is promised to the Church as one that will endure till the end. It will have to be considered presently what practical conclusions follow from this fundamental idea, which is based on the papal teaching about spiritual gifts and immediate relationship to Christ on one hand, and the institutional component of the Church on the other.

We must add another remark here concerning the texts quoted above. Spiritual gifts need not necessarily and in every case occur in a miraculously extraordinary form. Every genuinely Christian life serves the Body of Christ, even if it is lived in an 'inconspicuous' (rather than 'unimportant') place in the Church. It is the charismatic features of the Church as a whole which must in addition be of a striking character. For the Church, of course, is to be by its inexhaustible plenitude of holiness a sign set on high among the nations, and itself the proof of her divine origin and mission, as the First Vatican Council taught (Denzinger, *Enchiridion Symbolorum,* No. 1794). St Paul too assumes the same (for example in Galatians 3:2), for by the charismata the pagan is to recognize and acknowledge in adoration that 'God is among you indeed'. But that does not mean that because the Church's charismatic character functions as a mark of credibility, the spiritual gifts in its individual members must necessarily be something extra-ordinary. Leaving everything else out of account, there is heroic fidelity in commonplace, everyday things, the miracle of balance that hides its own miraculous quality in the serenity of the obvious. The Church teaches that even the lasting of observance of the natural law, that is, of what belongs to the accomplishment of human nature as such in this world, requires a special help from God which in fact, ultimately speaking, men only receive from the grace of Christ. Consequently even the preservation of purely human moral excellence points, objectively speaking, to the power of grace. How much more, therefore, is this true of what exceeds the average manner of life such as is 'generally' led, even if this feature that goes beyond the average appears very simple and not particularly noticeable precisely because of, not in spite of, its extraordinary and therefore, in our case, charismatic character.

I cannot here expound the teaching of St Paul concerning spiritual gifts in the Church: see in particular 1 Corinthians 12-14; Romans 12:1-8; 16:1; Ephesians 4:1-16. The mere reference must suffice.[1] By way of summary of it, one might

---

[1] E.A. Allo, *Première Épître aux Corinthiens* (Paris, 1935), pp. 317-388; B. Maréchaux, *Les charismes du St. Esprit* (Paris, 1921); D. Th. C. IV, 1728-1781; D. B. Suppl. I, 1233-47; H. J. Brosch, *Charismen und Ämter*

perhaps say that, for Paul, ecclesiastical offices can be spiritual gifts, but there are others. He regards ministries and other functions in the Body of Christ which by their nature cannot be institutionally administered, in the same perspective as gifts and tasks which the Spirit distributes, supports and combines, despite their diversity, for the life and well-being of the one Body of Christ. But at all events, and this is what is decisive for our purpose, Paul does not recognize only spiritual gifts that are bound up with office, ministries that are gifts of the Spirit both as office and as pneumatic enablement to fulfil the office. He recognizes other spiritual gifts as well, and recognizes them as just as important for building up the Body of Christ. Furthermore, these special charismata need not necessarily always concern extraordinary mystical things. The simplest help, the most commonplace service can be a charisma of the Spirit. Another striking fact is that Paul does not oblige the theologian by distinguishing between a *gratia gratum faciens* and a *gratia gratis data*, that is, between a grace that makes its recipient himself intrinsically holy and pleasing to God, and a grace only given 'gratuitously' to someone for the benefit of others and the Church generally but which does not sanctify the recipient. Not that such a distinction is not possible and in many cases appropriate. Jesus himself, of course, drew attention to men who work miracles and yet displease him. But Paul does not make the distinction. On the contrary he only sees or only envisages the case where the charismata both sanctify the recipient and redound to the benefit of the whole Body of Christ simultaneously and reciprocally. It is a very evangelical way of looking at it. For how else could one truly sanctify oneself except by being

in der Urkirche (Bonn, 1951); O. Karrer, *Um die Einheit der Christen* (Frankfurt, 1953), pp. 50-90.

unselfish to others in the one Body of Christ by the power of the Spirit? And how could one fail to be sanctified if one faithfully takes up and fulfils one's real and true function in the Body of Christ? If both are done, and that by God's Spirit, inconspicuously perhaps but in a truly spiritual way, that for Paul is a charisma of the Spirit of the Church, and it belongs just as essentially to the body and life of the Church as the official ministries.

Since this is noted by Paul and it is really so very obvious that theologians in their treatises on the Church may simply say nothing whatever about it? Yet that is what they do. In the outstanding treatise on ecclesiology in the Spanish text-books of dogmatic theology by Joachim Salaverri, for example, which goes far beyond what is usual in Germany in content, precision and bibliographical information, there is not a word about the charismatic element in the Church. All we find is a refutation, and rightly, of the theory of Sohm that any juridical element in the Church is in contradiction to her original charismatic conception. Of course, the charismatic element in the Church is not denied by theologians' thinking they do not need to waste a word on it in their treatises on the Church. To them it seems too self-evident. But when supposedly obvious things are passed over in silence[2] or it is considered they are no doubt dealt with elsewhere and from other angles with other concepts, there is considerable danger of their being overlooked. That will become clearer when we raise the question what practical conclusions emerge

[2] In H. Haag, *Bibellexikon* (Einsiedeln, 1951, we read, col. 541: 'Yet the gifts of the Spirit do not belong to the essence of the Church. This is not primarily charismatic but institutional, that is to say, built up on the apostles and their authority.' One can see that the pope is after all more 'progressive' than a progressive biblical dictionary of this sort. Can that objectively false statement really be justified by saying that it presupposes a more restricted conception of the charismata than ours?

48

from what has been said.

Since these practical applications have unavoidably a certain critical character, I may perhaps point out beforehand the following, which is also stressed in the encyclical *Mystici Corporis*, and which represents the third proof that the charismatic element belongs to the essence of the Church: This charismatic element has aways, in fact, existed in the Church.

Unfortunately people have become accustomed to some extent to attributing to the early Church a certain charismatic endowment which is supposed to stand in contrast to the history of the later Church and not any longer to be found so often, and no longer to be so necessary (as Gregory the Great rather regretfully added even in his time). Now there is no doubt that the early days of an historical structure, its first beginnings which are the foundation of all that comes later, have a unique task to fulfil, when something truly historic and with enduring identity is in question. The moment of first love is unique and irrecoverable, just as summer or autumn cannot be like spring. Even the mind's maturation in time cannot preserve eternal youth just as it is when one is really young. But the 'charismata of early days' and 'more charismata' are not the same thing. It is not clear what grounds there are for saying that the early Church was, in fact, more charismatic. Everything then was concentrated into a smaller space and consequently more noticeable. But even in the early Church not everything was charismatic enthusiasm. Moreover, the New Testament is an account which inevitably and quite rightly gives more attention to the great and holy events than to the human weaknesses that there certainly were even then. It goes without saying that as the Church grew, its 'machinery' grew too, and the regulations for this were worked out more fully. But this is no proof that in the early Church the wind of the Spirit blew with more vigour than later.

In fact, there has always been the charismatic element in the Church. We must glance into Church history, though more into the hidden everyday history than the official, 'great' Church history. If in doing so we reflect on fundamental principles rather than enumerate facts, that is legitimate within the framework of such considerations as these. Church history is not here being studied for its own sake.

The Spirit has always held sway anew in the Church, in ever new ways, always unexpectedly and creatively, and bestowed his gift of new life. He has never abolished official authority and laws, which after all derive from one and the same Spirit, but again and again brings them to fulfilment in ways other than those expected by the 'bureaucracy', the merely human side to office, which exists even in the Church. And he has again and again brought the hierarchy and the whole institutional element to recognize this influence of the Spirit. That is not the least of his repeated miracles. The love of martyrdom was a charisma which existed side by side in the early Church with cowardice, calculation and compromise. Charismata too were the numerous waves of monastic enthusiasm which led to ever new religious communities from Anthony and Pachomius down to the many smaller foundations of the nineteenth century, even if many such later foundations appear to have sprung more from shrewd, almost secular, aims and from a need for organization, than from an original impulse of the Spirit.

3. The possibility of institutional regulation of a gift of the Spirit

With regard to such charismatic enthusiasm for the evangelical counsels, which can only be followed through God's grace, it must be realized that not only the first emergence of such a mentality, which, of course, nearly always forestalls or occurs apart from and indeed, to all appearance, in spite of the institutional elements in the Church, but also the institutionally organized transmission and canalization of such gifts and graces of the Spirit, belong to the charismatic component of the Church. Not only Francis but the Franciscans too are charismatics if they really live in a spirit of joyous poverty. What would Francis mean to the Church if he had not found disciples throughout the centuries? He would not at all be the man of charismatic gifts in the sense we have in mind here, but a religious individualist, an unfortunate crank, and the world, the Church and history would have dropped him and proceeded with their business. But how could he possess disciples, many disciples, who have really written into the actual history of the Church something of the ever-young grace of the Spirit, if these disciples and the soul of the poor man of Assisi had refused on principle to be faithful to this Spirit of theirs under the yoke of ecclesiastical law, of statutes, vows and the obligation that derives from the liberty of love? It is precisely here that it is clear that the charismatic element belongs to the Church and to its very ministry as such. It has the courage, the astonishing and impressive courage, and many holders of office may well not realize what they are doing thereby, to regulate the charismatic element in the Church's life, to formulate 'laws' concerning it, and to 'organize' this Spirit. You have someone trying to do what according to the gospels is only possible by God's gift, what one can only 'take' if it is given from above, something that proclaims that the form of this world passes and that the last hour has already struck. He is offering his heart to God, that it may only think the things of God; telling God that in the adventure of love for him and as an expression of fath, he will renounce earthly love in marriage. He acknowledges this love for God. And the Church listens, receives this profession, administers it, binds the man who has made it, holds him to it in God's name. It is convinced, therefore, that the man who has made it has been taken at his word by God, that he truly possesses the charisma of Christian virginity. It knows, therefore, that God, because the Church does not release him from this obligation (which is after all that of his love), will also give him the grace to keep his promise. The Church lays down rules for such a life, makes a state of life out of this spiritual gift, similar to, or rather proportionately similar to the difference of status between the sacred ministry and those who hold no office. In the Latin Church it even combines its ministry and the state of life of celibate charismatics (at what a tremendous risk), and consecrates as its priests only those who declare in conscience before God that they have the grace to be able to take this venture upon themselves. It holds these consecrated servants of its sanctuary to their word and never releases them (though it could) from this obligation.

The Chuich must be very conscious indeed in this, its institutional and official activity, that it is the charismatic Church. In this it shows the sternness of exuberant life and the inexorability that it is a sacred necessity of the greatest things. It knows that only too often, as far as we can see, ultimate fulfilment and maturity are denied to such charismatic enthusiasm; that the holy venture of voluntary poverty, of a holy renunciation of earthly fulfilment, of contemplation in silence and obscurity, is only blessed with meagre fruits. And so it may sometimes seem as though the Church, harsh to the individual and his perhaps tragic lot, were only using such abundance of idealism for its own ends. It is not possible to

conceive the official Church and hierarchy as the institutional organizer and administrator of the gifts of the Spirit in the Church, unless one sees it from the start as being itself: the law-giving Church, first and foremost the Church of the charismata.

The sixteenth-century Reformers did not intend, of course, to reject the evangelical counsels as such, at least that was not the first intention; Scripture attests them too plainly. And it was only liberal rationalism of the eighteenth-century sort, with little understanding even of the faith of the Reformers, that thought itself obliged to be cleverer and wiser than Scripture in these matters. But what the Reformers could not see was that things of that kind could have anything to do with the visible Church and its officials and laws. They envisaged the Church in such a way that the hierarchy was really only a human form of organization, even if an unavoidable one, to meet religious needs. The Church of the later Middle Ages whose official ministries conducted themselves in a far from charismatic manner, did not make it easy for them to see it otherwise. And so for them spiritual 'office' properly speaking was only to be found where the gospel was preached in such a way that it pierced the heart in judgment and justification. A ministry of which even the theory was secularized in this way obviously could not claim to 'administer' the evangelical counsels which are a spiritual gift. On those premisses, such a rejection is understandable. If the ministry were no more than an institution belonging to this world (even though established by God, like the authority of the state, for example), it could not, in fact, 'administer' the free charismatic gifts of the Spirit. Anyone who can only see ecclesiastical office in that way, as an external expedient of an external order, and not as the efficacious sacrament of inward grace, cannot admit that the Church regulates and administers the evangelical counsels, but must deny that to follow them in the Church can constitute a 'state of life'.

4. Lesser and Greater Spiritual Gifts

To return, however, to the point I had reached in my

reflections. The Church throughout its history has always been charismatic. The excursus I have just made was perhaps not superfluous, if it has clarified what that means. For from that it follows that if the official Church is also the guardian and guide of the charismatic element, if itself possesses the gift of discernment of spirits, then the charismatic element is not to be looked for solely in what is very rare and extraordinary; that is practically beyond the reach of such guidance and only needs it in a very indirect and general way. It is not, of course, as if everything to do with God and his Spirit can and must be regulated and realized in the same way. There is certainly a domain which cannot be directly administered by the Church, but we cannot simply identify this with the realm of the spiritual gifts and so degrade the official Church into an external, bureaucratic, administrative machine. My excursus can serve to indicate that in the Church there is much more that is charismatic than one might at first think. How many human beings in the Church keep alight in the cloister the flame of prayer, adoration and silence? Is the intensity and magnitude of this phenomenon, even when one includes all its human and mediocre and ossified elements, all the dead wood, something to be taken for granted? Or is it astonishing, a grace and a miracle?

From this point our view broadens out into the history of the charismatic element in the Church and it becomes clearer that this seldom if ever means something that in the normal outlook of a secular historian would require to be given special prominence. It is not necessarily the case either, I hasten to add, that this grace-given charismatic element must necessarily be found only within the bounds of the visible Church. The idea of special spiritual gifts, at least when each individual case is viewed separately, does not include that of being an exclusive privilege. Consequently if in what follows I point out charismatic features in the Church and the impression is formed that such things after all exist outside the Church as well, and even outside Christianity, that is no argument against what has been said. For a Christian knows, confesses and feels it in no way a threat to the uniqueness and necessity of his Church, that there can be and is God's grace and the grace of Christ outside the Church. He does not prescribe to what heights that grace can raise a human being without, and before, incorporating him or her into the sacrament of grace, the Church. It is not even by any means settled in theology that any instance we observe anywhere in the world of the observance of the natural moral law, even in a single act, is, in fact, only a natural act without the supernatural elevating grace of Christ, even though it is not performed by a Christian from consciously supernatural motives. It is quite possible to hold that as a matter of fact in all or nearly all cases where a genuine spiritually and morally good action is actually accomplished, it is also, in fact, more than merely such an act. The grace of Christ surrounds man more than we think, and is deeper, more hidden and pervasive in its application in the depth of his being than we often imagine. It is quite conceivable that wherever a human being really affirms moral values as absolutely binding, whether expressly or merely in the actual unreflecting accomplishment of his nature, intrinsically orientated as this is beyond and above itself towards the absolute mystery of God, he possesses that attitude of authentic faith (even if only virtually), which together with love, suffices for justification and so makes possible supernatural acts that positively conduce to eternal life.

If this is taken into account, it becomes even clearer that we have no right to assign arbitrary limits to the grace of God outside the Church and so make spiritual gifts and favours simply and solely an exclusive privilege of the Church alone. But on the other hand this does not mean, either, that we are not permitted to see the charismatic element in the Church where it really exists within it, not in the great pages that belong to general world history merely, but in hidden fidelity, unselfish kindness, sincerity of disposition and purity of heart, virile courage that does a duty without fuss; in the uncompromising profession of truth, even when it is invidious; in the inexpressible love of a soul for God; in the unshakable trust of a sinner that God's heart is greater than ours and that he is rich in mercy. All that and very much more of the same kind is by the grace of God what it really is, and what only the believer can correctly appreciate in its full profundity and endless significance, for the unbeliever underestimates it. It is the work of grace and not of the human heart, which of itself alone would be evil, cowardly and empty.

Now are there not things of that kind everywhere in the Church, over and over again? Have we any right to observe morosely that they really ought to be even greater, more splendid and more powerful? At bottom, of course, we often don't want to see or experience such greater things out of genuine love of these holy possibilities of mankind, but because we ourselves would have a more comfortable and agreeable time in life if there were even more of such divine goodness in the world. Isn't it often rather our own egoism we should blame for our being so blind to the splendid things there are, that we act as though it were all a matter of course, or of no importance? If we had real humility and goodness we would see far more marvels of goodness in the Church. But because we are selfish ourselves, we are only ready to see good, good brought about by God, where it suits our advantage, our need for esteem, or our view of the Church. But this unrecognized goodness, and even charismatic goodness, is found in the Church in rich abundance. That is not altered by the fact that more is brought into God's barns than is consigned in the pages of newspapers, and magazines, histories of civilization and other such human halls of fame. Can it not be charismatic goodness to be a patient nursing sister, serving, praying, and asking nothing else of life? That does not mean it is always so. Nor need one fail to recognize that even genuine virtue is rooted in temperament, social origins, custom and other pre-moral conditions, just as a beautiful flower grows from mould. But only a blind and malicious mind can no longer see, on account of the imperfection of all human things, or because of the facile discovery that even the most authentic moral excellence has its antecedent non-moral conditions, that despite all that and in it all, there can be charismatic goodness and love, fidelity and courage.

Persons of that kind, who cannot thankfully admire this goodness effected by the Spirit in the Church, and outside it, might inquire whether they themselves accomplish the things they refuse to think remarkable. Consider a mother's life. It is no doubt true that she has a narrow outlook, instinctive care for offspring drives her on; probably she would not have a much better time in this life if she were not so devoted a mother. That and more of the same kind may be true and in many cases is true. But just as life on the biological level presupposes chemistry, yet is more than chemistry (even though many theorists fail to see this), so it is, proportionately speaking, in these matters. There are good mothers whose virtue is from God above, a gift of the Spirit and of his unselfish love. And there are many such gifts of the Spirit that are the charismata in the Church. The ones mentioned are only meant as isolated examples. It is in these that the life that most truly characterizes the Church is accomplished, not in culture, the solution of social questions, ecclesiastical politics, the learned treatises of theologians, but in faith, hope and love, in the longing for eternity, the patience of the Cross, heartfelt joy. Ultimately the whole Church is only there so that such things may exist, so that

witness may be borne to their eternal significance, so that
there may always be people who really and seriously believe
that these gifts here on earth and hereafter in eternity are
more important than anything else. It remains true, of
course, that men are frequently required to do these apparently small things of eternity among apparently greater
temporal matters. And it is true that what has been said must
not be made a pretext and easy excuse for narrow-minded
mediocrities who lack this and that quality but flatter themselves that they are citizens and philistines on this earth, and
who want to award the 'common man' a halo that he doesn't
deserve in a matter where a more aristocratic awareness of
difference of level and achievement would be more authen-
tically human.

Of course, if it were a question of writing a history of the
charismatic element in the Church, one would have to speak
more explicitly than has so far been done here about the
great spiritual gifts, about the great saints in whose creative
example quite new possibilities of Christian life can be seen;
about the great figures of Church history who walked like
true guides and shepherds before the people of God on its
journey through this world of time and led it into new
historical epochs, often without realizing themselves what
they were doing, like Gregory the Great who himself was
expecting the end of the world and yet became the father of
the Middle Ages in the West. Of the great thinkers and
writers, too, who took up again the ancient Christian view of
life and succeeded in so expressing it that a new age could
make that Christianity its own. And the great artists who did
not speak about the religion in which God became a man of
this earth, but gave it visible shape, representing it in ever
new forms and so actually and concretely represented something which, without such corporeal embodiment, only too
easily asphyxiates the mere depths of conscience or evaporates

as it were into unreality in the abstractions of the mind. In other words, one would have to speak of all in the Church who had a special, unique historical mission of great import for the Church and through it for the world. It goes without saying that no detailed account can be given here of all these great charismata.

Now, to add another fundamental observation, these charismata are not only properties of the Church's essence which only the eye of faith perceives (all the charismata are that), but they are also criteria that convince and lead to faith, by which the Church is to be recognized as a work of God. This is not the place to go into the difficult question, one of the most important questions of fundamental theology, how and on what presuppositions such criteria of true belief can be recognized by human reason, which, in faith, has to perform a 'reasonable service', *rationabile obsequium*. What is the rôle and scope of reason and of deliberate reflection expressible in rational terms; what is the function of grace; how do the light of faith and rational grounds of faith mutually support one another in the actual accomplishment of faith? This general problem has a particular application here from the fact that the charismatic element in the Church is not only an object of faith but by its plenitude and enduring presence and its perpetually renewed vitality, can be a motive of faith. Here we can only stress this fact. The first Vatican Council, taking up a thesis of Cardinal Deschamps, emphasizes (Denzinger, 1794) that 'The Church itself is a great and enduring motive of credibility and an irrefutable testimony to its divine mission by its wonderful growth, eminent holiness and inexhaustible fruitfulness in all good, and by its Catholic unity and unshakable stability.' By the nature of the case this implies that the great charismata of the Church in its temporal and spatial unity and totality, in which these gifts appear to the gaze of the unprejudiced as a special characteristic of it, are not only an object of faith but a motive of faith.

Of course, the use of this motive of faith in apologetics is not perfectly easy. The matter cannot, however, be pursued here. We discern the limits of something that was emphasized earlier, that there are gifts of the Spirit even outside the one visible Church. What I have said does not, however, mean that the situation of the Church is simply the same as that of the Christian and non-Christian world outside the Church. The eye of faith and the human mind seeking faith with the support of grace can recognize that the charismata which are found everywhere have, nevertheless, in the Church their home and native air and their most intense historical development, because more than any other historical entity it proves itself to be, again and again and ever anew, the Church of the great charismata.

5. The Consequences

a. Toleration of a charisma by offical authority

If the structure of the Church is of this double kind and if its harmonious unity is ultimately guaranteed only by the one Lord, then office-holders and institutional bodies must constantly remind themselves that it is not they alone who rule in the Church. We have already sufficiently emphasized that God's Spirit will ensure that they do not rule in that way and in decisive matters will not wish to do so. But this fact in no way means that temptations to the contrary never arise or that such a maxim is superfluous because its final accomplishment is guaranteed. Neither the efficacious grace given in God's salvific acts nor the indefectible promise to the Church of the assistance of the Holy Spirit renders such a maxim superfluous. It is important for office-holders and their subjects, too, to keep it clearly before their minds. Both must realize that in the Church which has this charismatic element, subordinates are quite definitely not simply people who have to carry out orders from above. They have other commands as well to carry out, those of the Lord himself who also guides his Church directly and does not always in the first place convey his commands and promptings to ordinary Christians through the ecclesiastical authorities, but has entirely reserved for himself the right to do this directly in a great variety of ways that have little to do with keeping to the standard procedure and the 'usual channels'.

In the Church there are not only movements that have to owe their origin to higher authority in order to be legitimate. The official hierarchy must not be surprised or annoyed if there is stirring in the life of the spirit before this has been scheduled in the Church's ministries. And subordinates must not think they have nothing definite to do until an order is handed down from above. There are actions that God wills even before the starting signal has been given by the hierarchy, and in directions that have not yet been positively approved and laid down officially. Canon law concerning equity and the force of custom *contra* or *praeter legem* might be thought out from the point of view of this charismatic element in the Church. By such concepts canonists not only leave legitimate room for humanly significant development in the law, but also for the impulse of the Spirit, even if and in spite of the fact that these points in the Church's body can also, of course, become the focus of infection by the all-too-human element. Executive authority in the Church must, therefore, always cultivate the awareness that it is not, and may not be, the self-sufficient planner, as though in a totalitarian system, of all that is done in the Church. It must keep alive the consciousness that it is a duty and not a gracious condescension when it accepts suggestions from 'below';

that it must not from the start pull all the strings; and that the higher and, in fact, charismatic wisdom can sometimes be with the subordinate, and that the charismatic wisdom of office may consist in not shutting itself off from such higher wisdom. Ecclesiastical authority must always realize that a subject's duty of obedience, and the fact that such authority has competence to determine what its competence is, neither makes the subordinate devoid of rights as against authority, nor guarantees that every action of authority in the individual case is correct and the one willed by God.

b. The 'democratic' Church

Seeing that there is a divinely-willed dualism of charisma and office of a permanent kind in the Church, then, the 'monarchical' Church, with its authority deriving from above downwards, has, nevertheless, also something of the nature of a democracy — the opposite of a totalitarian system. The name does not matter and nowadays to some people the word democracy will not seem a special title of honour, seeing that everybody everywhere is supposedly in favour of democracy even if we in the West use it to mean precisely the opposite of what is called by that name elsewhere. But if we do consider what ultimately constitutes a democracy, it is, of course, not a voting paper in everybody's hand (for those voting papers when collected together can be very tyrannical), but a society where no single authority holds all power combined, where there is a plurality of really distinct powers, so that the individual always knows he is protected to some extent by one from the excessive power of the other. In this sense every healthy state has been a pluralist state and consequently to that extent democratic. Under any constitution such a concentration of power can occur that, in fact, freedom is abolished, though that is not to say that it is equally easy, whatever the written constitution, for freedom to be abolished by a monopoly of power.

This helps us to a better grasp of what characterizes the Church's constitution. It is 'undemocratic' because its office and authority, being founded directly by God himself, have for mankind final jurisdiction in their own domain. There is no absolute right to resistance or need for it in that domain, because God himself guarantees that the authority will not abuse its formal rights in a materially decisive way. But there is not on that account in the Church any absolute monopoly of real power at any one point, that is, in this case, in its hierarchy. Not because that sort of thing is, in fact, never altogether feasible (it is not so even in the cruellest and most ruthless tyranny), but because it is contrary to the very nature and purpose of the Church as embodied in its ministry itself. This does not aim even on principle and in intention at gathering to itself all real influence. It sets limits to itself and this limitation which allows due scope to other forces of a non-official kind is itself guaranteed by God. To that extent, therefore, the Church is a hierarchical system, but only because its summit is God, and likewise a system in which power and authority are distributed, that is, a sort of democracy though of its own special kind.

From what has been said it is clear that even in the Church, something can originate from among the people. Not from the people of this earth merely, but from the people of God in the Church, the people of God that is guided directly by God. Consequently there is also quite rightly something in the Church of the nature of a popular element. A religious study of this popular element that regarded itself as a genuine theological study could begin at this point to define its nature and importance. To the extent that the host of believers, where it is united in heart and soul, can be the point of entry for guidance from above, it is possible in certain circumstances to discern the Spirit of the Church in it and in what it does and feels. It, of course, remains true and goes without saying that this people is the people of God, existing in the society of the Church organized by Christ, and consequently can never stand in fundamental contradiction to the ecclesiastical authority which gives it social form and structure. There have repeatedly been times in the Church's history, the eighteenth-century Enlightenment, for example, when many a gift of God's Spirit to his Church was better preserved by this simple and prayerful people than by many of the 'princes of the Church'.

c. Inevitable disagreement in the Church

If by her very nature there is necessarily a multiplicity of impulsions in the Church, then a legitimate opposition of forces is not only, in fact, unavoidable, but is to be expected and must be accepted by all as something that should exist. It is not just to be regarded as a necessary evil. Only impulses that in the human sphere flow from a single source cannot be felt to be 'dialectical', opposed. But when in the Church's case various influences flow from God into the Church, some through the ministry, others directly to members of the Church who hold no office, it is clear that God alone can fully perceive the meaning, direction and divinely-willed purpose of these. If for no other reason than that man, being finite even as a member of the Church, makes his place in relation to what he cannot foresee. A number of forces like this within the Church here on earth must be felt by human beings themselves as disparate and opposed, precisely because they are unified by God alone. Of course, it is true, as Paul says, that the various gifts of the one Spirit must work together harmonious in the unity of the one Body of Christ. But since the gifts are one in the one Spirit but do not form one gift, that unity of the Body of Christ itself is only fully one in the one Spirit. For the rest it is true that no one singly forms the whole. No one has every function. Whatever the breadth and the will to wholeness, to understanding, to assimilation, the plurality of special gifts cannot be abolished.

Ultimately only one thing can give unity in the Church on the human level: the love which allows another to be different, even when it does not understand him. This makes it more understandable that charity is not only present in the Church as though in a container, but itself belongs to the actual constitutive elements of the Church, in contradistinction to all other societies. For only then can the Church be one in spite of its dual structure. The principle that charity brings with it implies that each in the Church may follow his spirit as long as it is not established that he is yielding to what is contrary to the Spirit; that, therefore, orthodoxy, freedom and goodwill are to be taken for granted and not the opposite. Those are not only self-evident human maxims of a sensible common life built on respect and tolerance for others, but also principles which are very deeply rooted in the very nature of the Church and must be so. For they follow from the fact that the Church is not a totalitarian system. Patience, tolerance, leaving another to do as he pleases as long as the error of his action is not established — and not the other way round, prohibition of all individual initiative until its legitimacy has been formally proved, with the onus of proof laid on the subordinate — are, therefore, specifically ecclesiastical virtues springing from the very nature of the Church. We have an example of this attitude in the *Codex Iuris Canonici*, canon 1323, § 3: It must be proved not presumed that a theological proposition has been solemnly defined.

We must learn, then, even as members of the Church, to

65

let others be, even when we do not understand them, even when one has the 'feeling' that they don't think as one 'really' should, that is, according to one's own particular dispositions. It follows that there must be schools and trends in theology, in the spiritual life, in church art and in pastoral practice. Anyone who does not admit this is tacitly asserting that there could be a place in the Church from which all those matters were directed in detail, authoritatively, in a way binding on all and in all, so that all other persons would be merely the executors (and of a most passive and repetitive sort) of quite definite detailed views and commands. But that is just what is not the case. Even in theology it is not so; even, that is, in theory, which after all is more susceptible of unanimity than practical matters are. Of course, there are always naïve and over-enthusiastic souls whose secret wish and ideal is, in fact, represented by what the opponents of papal infallibility at the time of the first Vatican Council always painted on the wall of their untheological imaginations as a nightmare danger, namely that the infallible pope might simply settle all theological questions by his infallible pronouncement. One should ask oneself for once just why, strictly speaking, that really will not do, seeing that after all he has authority for something of the sort. If one attentively considers the simple and rather foolish question, one realizes that it is really the case, as we noted above, that the plenary powers of the highest authority in the Church, which are not subject to the check of any other human court of appeal, are not by any means the whole source from which, and in accordance with which, that highest authority acts. There belongs to it too the assistance of the Holy Spirit, which cannot be completely expressed in juridical terms, and his guidance in the actual exercise of those plenary powers. Moreover, in the present case it has to be noted too that human truth in fact is of such a kind that even in theology to settle one question, even correctly, raises three new questions that remain to be settled. Only simple-minded people fail to realize that, and think the pope, if he were only willing, could change dogmatic theology into a collection of defined propositions. For that matter it is only necessary to glance into church history to see that there has never been a trend in the Church which in the long run was wholly and solely right and triumphed to the exclusion of all others. And trends or programmes only put themselves completely in the wrong when they put themselves outside the Church in schism. One alone has always been completely right, the one Lord of the Church who, one in himself, has willed the many opposing tendencies in the Church.

What has been said would be quite misunderstood if anyone drew the conclusion that everything in the Church must be left to go its way, that no one may have the courage to offer opposition to another trend in the Church, to utter warnings against it, to challenge it to real and serious combat. Such a view would, of course, amount to denying that the different kinds of movements and tendencies truly do develop within the one Church so that each must be balanced by the others. It would also involve maintaining that no tendencies can appear in the Church except as a gift of the Holy Spirit. But this is false. So we must also be able to have the courage (for this can be the precise function given by the Spirit to a particular member of the Church), to say No in the Church, to make a stand against certain trends and spirits, even before the official hierarchy itself has been alarmed. In fact, such a protest can be God's means of rousing his ministers to act. One must have this courage, even if one must tell oneself, knowing the limits of one's own judgment, that probably the further history of the Church will show that one was not entirely right, that one was only one servant among many of the one Lord of the Church, and not the only one to

67

represent him, in fact, that the Lord was also acting in that other person whom one had the task of putting in his place, and convincing of his limitations.

d. The burden of a charisma

That is why a charisma always involves suffering. For it is painful to fulfil the task set by the charisma, the gift received, and at the same time within the one body to endure the opposition of another's activity which may in certain circumstances be equally justified. One's own gift is always limited and humbled by another's gift. Sometimes it must wait until it can develop until its *kairos*, its hour has come, when that of another has passed or is fading. This painful fact is to be viewed soberly as an inevitable consequence of there being one Church and many gifts. If the words are taken seriously and not emptied of meaning, 'many gifts' implies that one person has a gift that another has not. How could that other person show an understanding of a gift that is only possible to its possessor who is called to exercise that precise function in the Church? Even supposing we had all the goodwill and tolerance that we could or should have, it would still not be possible to show another and his gift and task that understanding and enthusiasm which he expects and is tempted to claim his mission justifies and requires. Outside the Church the man with a mission may, of course, be misunderstood and persecuted, but he can flee to those who esteem him and recognize his mission and a community can be founded and centred on this mission. In the Church this is only possible to a much more limited extent, for example by the founding of an order or similar social structures in the Church which are legitimate and derive part of their meaning and justification from this need for social response to a new mission. In general someone in the Church who bears the burden of a charismatic mission to the Church and for the Church, must remain in the circle of his brethren. They will tolerate him when things go well but perhaps reject him and in any case show little understanding of him. The authenticity of a charisma, which after all is for the Church and into the Church, not out of her, is shown by the fact that the person so endowed bears humbly and patiently this inevitable sorrow of his charismatic endowment, builds no little chapel for himself inside the Church in order to make things more tolerable, does not become embittered but knows that it is the one Lord who creates a force and resistance to it, the wine of enthusiasm and the water of sobriety in his Church, and has given to none of his servants singly the task of representing him.

Two observations must be made on this theme of the burden of a spiritual gift in the Church. One is, that to suffer opposition to the charisma within the Church is no proof against the mission from above and the authenticity of the gift. Certainly the Church has the right and duty of discernment of spirits even to the point of completely rejecting a claim that this or that spirit is from God. But that does not mean that every contradiciton, delay, distrust that is aroused in the Church or its authorities against a charisma is itself a sign that this prophet has not been sent by Yahweh. The criteria for distinguishing between thc legitimate opposition of the Church to a deceitful spirit and false enthusiasm on one hand and, the painful resistance of the Church to the mission of its own Spirit in a true 'prophet' on the other, are known in their main features and need not be expounded in more detail here. They are the rules which the Church and its theology lay down regarding its teaching authority, its various levels and their binding force, and the equally discriminating rules about ecclesiastical obedience. In this respect another thing must be said. To apply these rules correctly in more difficult cases is itself a charisma, a special gift. For who can tell always and at once, precisely and definitely, when self-defence of a charismatic mission against the mistrust, difference or hesitation of holders of ecclesiastical office, or even against their actual opposition, is a sign of higher charismatic insight and fidelity to his own mission, and when an attitude of illegitimate revolt against ecclesiastical authority? Why, for example, were the Jesuits right in acting as they did when they resisted Pius V's attempt to impose solemn choir-office on them? Why were they not breaking their own rules of thinking with the Church? Why was it a praiseworthy action on the part of the representatives of devotion to the Sacred Heart not to allow themselves to be put off by the rejection which they first met with from the Holy See? How often can one really remonstrate with the competent authority with petitions, pressure and so on, without by that very fact offending against the ecclesiastical spirit? When is as minimizing an interpretation as possible of an ecclesiastical prohibition, in order to continue to preserve as much room and freedom of movement for an endeavour that has the appearance of contradicting it, quite definitely compatible (as even the practice of the saints shows), with an ecclesiastical spirit, and when not? Such questions show (and that was their only purpose here), that it can itself be a special gift given only to the humble and brave, obedint yet independent and responsible saint, to discern where the burden of opposition to a mission is the cross which blesses a genuine mission and where it is a proof that the endeavour has not its origin in God. There are too it is clear that it is not possible completely to comprise in plain rules of law the stirrings of the Church's life, that a charismatic element remains.

The second thing to be said about the burden of a charisma is that the inner necessity that links charisma and suffering in the Church, of course gives no patent to the authorities, and others devoid of special gifts, to be lacking in understanding, and blind and obstinate. Sometimes one has the impression that there are people in the Church who infer from Gamaliel's words (Acts 5:38 ff.), that the authenticity of the Spirit is shown by its not being extinguished by the most frivolous and malicious opposition from other people, and that consequently they have the right to put the spirit to the test on the largest possible scale. Of course, it is not possible to extinguish the Spirit in the Church, God sees to that. But it is quite possible for a human being by his sloth and indifference and hardness of heart to extinguish a true spirit in another. Not only is it possible for grace to be without fruit in the person for whom it is intended, through his own resistance, but it can be given to someone for another's benefit — it is then called *gratia gratis data* or *charisma* — and remain without fruit because rejected by the person for whom it was given, although it was faithfully received by the one who received it on another's behalf. We must not be Jansenists in our doctrine of the charismata, either, and hold that all these special gifts must be given as *gratiae efficaces*, infallibly producing their effect. There are also gifts which through men's fault remain without effect for the Church. Gamaliel for that matter drew from his maxim the contrary conclusion to that of the people we have in mind. He inferred that one must be as tolerant as possible towards a spirit whose origin one cannot yet clearly make out. Ecclesiastical authorities cannot, therefore, do wrong on the grounds that a spirit will triumph in the end even against their opposition, if it really comes from God. Otherwise they cause suffering beyond what is unavoidable, do wrong to God, to those endowed with spiritual gifts and to the Church.

Anyone even slightly familiar with the history of the Church knows of sufficient examples of suffering of that kind by those gifted by the Spirit. St John of the Cross was thrown into a horrible dungeon by his own brethren, St Joan of Arc died at the stake, Newman lived for years under a cloud, Sailer of Ratisbon was denigrated in Rome by another saint, Clement Maria Hofbauer, and only became a bishop when it was really too late, Mary Ward was for a long time in the custody of the Inquisition and yet, of course, she was right about her mission, nevertheless. In the controversy about the nature of the love of God, Fénelon was disavowed, not without reason, by Rome, but his adversary Bossuet who seemed to have triumphed was not much nearer the truth than his less powerful opponent. In her foundations St Teresa of Jesus, certainly to her great sorrow, had to undergo much persecution on the part of ecclesiastics, and use much ingenuity and many ruses in order to succeed. From the beginning of the Church down to the present day there have been great and small instances, of these and similar kinds, of the sufferings of the charismatic individual, and there will continue to be. They are unavoidable. They belong to the inescapable 'necessity' of suffering by which Christ continues to suffer in his members until the end. And he willed that these his members should also cause on another to suffer.

e. The courage to receive new gifts

A final remark by way of conclusion. One must learn to perceive such charismata when they first appear. Jesus himself observed that the children of those who killed the prophets put up monuments to them, but this did not reconcile him to the prophets' fate. It is good and has its uses if the prophets are renowned and canonized when they are dead and their charisma has been officially recognized. But it is almost of greater importance to perceive such gifts of the Spirit on their first appearance so that they may be furthered and not choked by the incomprehension and intellectual laziness, if not the ill-will and hatred, of those around them, ecclesiastics included. That is not very easy. For the institution is always the same and develops, to the extent that it does develop, from the palpable, unambiguous principles it embodies from the outset — though this is not to dispute the creative and spontaneous element even in the juridical development of the Church, at least in its *ius humanum*. But the charismatic is essentially new and always surprising. Of course it also stands in inner though hidden continuity with what came earlier in the Church and fits in with its spirit and with its institutional framework. Yet it is new and incalculable, and it is immediately evident at first sight that everything is as it was in the enduring totality of the Church. For often it is only through what is new that it is realized that the range of the Church was greater from the outset than had previously been supposed. And so the charismatic feature, when it is new, and one might almost say it is only charismatic if it is so, has something shocking about it. It can be mistaken for facile enthusiasm, a hankering after change, attempted subversion, lack of feeling for tradition and the well-tried experience of the past. And precisely those who are firmly rooted in the old, who have preserved a living Christianity as a sacred inheritance from the past, are tempted to extinguish the new spirit, which does not always fix on what is most tried and tested, and yet may be a holy spirit for all that, and to oppose it in the name of the Church's Holy Spirit, although it is a spiritual gift of that Spirit.

PART III

Some criteria for genuine visions

Here I shall try to deduce some criteria for genuine visions and thus to some extent supply criteria for the attitude to be adopted when psychic phenomena occur which purport to be genuine visions and revelations of God.

First of all which are the unsatisfactory or at least inadequate criteria? Piety and personal honesty are absolutely perequisite before a vision can possibly claim to be considered genuine, but are no proof of its authenticity because these qualities are no protection against error. Even saints have frequently been deceived in such matters.

The same is true of (bodily and) mental health. The argument from health tacitly assumes that if the vision is not 'genuine', then the visionary must be hysterical or mad. But as the visionary otherwise gives the impression of being perfectly normal and rational by conventional standards, it is concluded (unless for other reasons the question of diabolical influence arises) that the vision must be authentic. This argument, for several reasons, is false or inconclusive. For one thing it overlooks the fact that a sharply defined insanity may affect a part of mental life in isolation from the rest, which latter appears to remain quite normal. Furthermore it assumes that all phenomena which do not occur in the ordinary mental life of a rational western man must be either pathological or the effect of a transcendent cause. This presupposition, however, is false. There are phenomena which on the one hand are natural and not pathological, and, on the other hand, are not caused by any transcendent influence: spontaneous eidetic experiences, extraordinary achievements which cannot be produced at will but emerge from the subconscious, moments of brilliant intellectual accomplishment which seem literally inspired from without and from above — things, in short, beyond the ken of the average man of our time, which are neither 'normal', nor really 'anomalous', nor supernatural. Even where no supernatural agency is involved, 'extraordinary' and 'pathological' are not synonymous terms. In short, merely because a visionary is sane it does not follow that he must have 'authentic' visions.

Neither clarity nor stability nor apparent objectivity conclusively prove a vision genuine, but may at times indicate the opposite. Furthermore it should be noted that elements of the total vision which belong to the realm of parapsychological, mediumistic powers must not be taken for decisive criteria. If genuine (natural) telepathy, telaesthesia, cryptaesthesia, and even physical mediumistic powers exist (and such possibilities must at least be seriously reckoned with), then we must disregard many phenomena formerly, perhaps, accepted as decisive proofs of the supernatural origin of visions. It would still be necessary, of course, to allow for the possibility of God's supernatural intervention using these mediumistic powers for his own purposes or setting them in involuntary operation as happens with other human faculties. Many extraordinary phenomena in the lives of the saints might be thus explained.

Personal integrity is continually cited as a criterion of authenticity. In fact it seems difficult, especially in personal encounter with the visionary, not to be swayed by this 'test' of personal influence. Père Tonquédec, with his vast experience as an exorcist in Paris, strongly advises against concluding that a vision must be genuine if the visionary is sincere and seems incapable of deceiving anyone. We have already seen that even obviously good effects are no absolute criterion. Staehlin also draws attention to what is known as 'transfiguration', where the features are transformed by an 'unearthly' beauty. He reports a case in his own experience where he observed a girl during an ecstasy, and then withdrew because of the crowd. When she had recovered from the ecstasy he failed to recognize her. Only by her clothes was he able to convince himself of her identity. Her face, destitute of radiance, was perfectly commonplace. Other onlookers even spoke of her clothes shining, and one person who had always refused to believe in apparitions before was quite convinced by this experience. Yet it was a case of ordinary hallucination.

As to positive criteria, it will be well to distinguish between standards for the visionary himself and those for outside observers.

Even for the visionary the impression of real sensory perception is no apodictic criterion. However, if the imaginative vision is connected with a proper and original mystical phenomenon belonging to the realm of infused contemplation, then it is quite possible that the visionary, in the act of this experience, may be unable to doubt its divine origin, thus finding a warranty for the truth of his imaginative vision insofar as the two things are cause and effect. After such a mystical vision the seer may, by reflecting on the central mystical experience in the light of criteria which we need not discuss here, attain a secondary certitude that he has really had that experience. It would then be permissible to assume that the imaginative vision has also been a true one. Detailed analysis would still, of course, have to reckon with subjective elements in the whole content of the vision, such as possible misinterpretations and faulty recollection.

But in every case, according to the doctors of mystical

theology, one should take the attitude that visions are relatively unimportant compared with the infused contemplation from which they derive, and compared with faith, charity and the other supernatural Christian virtues, which should be our principal concern. Where there is neither infused contemplation nor an external miracle to authenticate the vision, the seer will scarcely be justified, in practice, in accepting it without qualification as genuine. If the vision contains nothing offensive to faith and Christian morals, if it fosters his spiritual progress without inducing him to give it undue importance for his personal religious life and to assume the rôle of a prophet sent to others, he must either suspend definitive judgment on the vision or else accept it in humility, in gratitude, and in silence[1] as an aid to his own devotion.

As for *us*, outside observers, if it is a matter of purely mystical visions which do not claim a prophetic mission the same criteria will apply, *mutatis mutandis*, which we have established for the visionary himself. But, as we cannot directly observe the interior, mystical experience of infused contemplation in the seer and it will be less certain or less probable (for us) that it really has occurred, our power to arrive at reasonable certainty, through the use of the same criteria, though not nullified will be seriously diminished.

In practice, then (failing the external evidence of a miracle) we must content ourselves with more or less probability and

[1] May not the fact that in almost all series of apparitions a secret is communicated about which absolutely nothing must be said, indicate a consciousness of the duty of silence when a person has visionary experiences? — The answer of Lucia and of the two other children to the questions of Canon Formigão gives the distinct impression that a personal secret must have been involved. It is 'for the good of the three of us' (Jacinta, p. 92); it concerns 'all three' (Lucia, p. 75); 'it is for the good of his own soul, and for Lucia's and Jacinta's' (Francisco, p. 106).

accord a mystical vision of the respect due to the spiritual life of sane and devout people. Whether what the visionary saw does or does not have a meaning for one's own spiritual life is a matter for one's own free judgment.

Certainly there is no obligation to attach much importance to such things when classic mystical doctrine warns the visionary himself against attributing too much value or significance to these experiences. Where they are alleged by people without the properly mystical graces of infused contemplation, it can almost always be safely assumed that such visions (if not fraudulent or pathological) are para-psychological, eidetic or other hallucinatory or pseudo-hallucinatroy occurrences. For, on the other hand, these phenomena can occur in people who are morally and mentally sound and, on the other hand, they adequately account for the facts of the case. The principle always remains valid that supernatural agency is not to be presupposed but must be proved. The history of mysticism justifies Poulain's judgment that even with pious and 'normal' people, in three cases out of four visions are well intentioned, harmless, genuine illusions.[2] With such occurrences, therefore, there is more danger of error in credulity than in scepticism, especially in unsettled times.

But where we encounter 'prophetic' visions, which lay demands upon us the validity and binding force of which are not

[2] This seems also to have been the opinion of St Paul of the Cross: in a letter he tells the amusing little story that St Theresa once appeared to a nun and told her: 'Know that of all the visions and auditions . . . that I myself have had, only a small part, a very small part was true and good' (*RAM* viii [1927], p. 383); indeed he even writes in one letter (*ibid.*, p. 381) 'amongst hundreds or perhaps thousands of these articulated auditions, scarcely one or two are true.' It is well to remember that St Paul of the Cross himself enjoyed very advanced mystical graces.

not evident apart from these visions, the only criterion which can justify this claim is a real miracle (physical or moral) in the strict sense.

If Catholic fundamental theology can and must apply this criterion to public Christian revelation, how much more must it apply to private prophetic revelations. Demands, messages — even within the framework of general revealed doctrine — direct to others than the visionary himself and based on a vision, must prove their divine origin and their binding character by miracles. But even then they will not generally call for the belief of *fides divina*[1] like public revelation (certainly not for *fides catholica*), if only because it is clear (as it is in the case of public revelation) that God is prepared to grant everybody the graces of light and strength which are necessary for such acts of faith. Without a miracle such a vision can lay no claim whatever to the assent of outsiders.[2] To reject such a revelation (always conformably to our general human duty of caution, restraint, and reverence) in any case never implies resistance to divine grace, and may rather be part of man's duty to 'believe not every spirit; but try the spirits if they be of God'.

[1] It is the common teaching of theologians that the authenticity of a private revelation may be so clear for the visionary himself that he is permitted and even bound to believe its content with divine faith. Cf., e.g., Dieckmann, *De ecclesia* II (Freiburg, 1952), pp. 150 f.

[2] These miracles, however, must not themselves raise a problem, like the miracle of the sun, which was not by any means seen by all those present. Thus Izabel Brandão de Melo writes in a letter dated October 13, 1917: 'this (the report of the sun-miracle) is what people were saying next to me, and what thousands of persons claim they saw. I did not see it, although I looked at the sun and felt terribly moved to hear everybody screaming that they saw extraordinary things in the sun ....' Cf. L. G. da Fonseca, *Fátima y la crítica*, p. 18 and note 27. Nevertheless, this witness believed in the apparitions. Father Martindale in his book *The message of Fátima* (p. 82) speaks of two English ladies who did not see the sun-miracle either (cf. Fonseca, *ibid.*).

If the investigations and the judgment of the Church declare that a particular vision and private revelation may be believed with human faith (for the Church does no more than this), this ecclesiastical approbation in itself is not necessarily infallible (for the infallible magisterium was not given to the Church, the custodian of general public revelation in Christ, for this purpose). The approbation implies only that such a revelation can show good grounds for human credibility and does not contradict the deposit of faith; like all important acts of the Church's pastoral authority (to which this judgment is to be attributed rather than to the magisterium), it deserves to be respectfully obeyed by the faithful. (Nothing more is necessary, by the very nature of the judgment, which imposes virtually no activity on the faithful). Yet a Catholic is not forbidden to think within himself, for weighty reasons, that the judgment is in fact incorrect; and if he feels it appropriate he may even express his opinion with becoming modesty, always provided this will not promote an attitude of general scepticism which ultimately would deny the possibility of any supernatural, historical revelation of God. Much more will a critical attitude be permissible towards the details of a vision which, as a whole, is recognized as genuine.

And even if a vision (mystical or prophetic) be recognized in itself as genuine, our attitude towards it, our reaction to it may still be wrong. One may be deaf, or refractory, to the message. Who can deny that most people do not welcome a call to penance or a devotion that would be salutary for a given time? But the other extreme is also possible, especially among people of a piety too intuitive and unenlightened. Where private revelations (even genuine ones) are abused to gratify a spiritual sensationalism, those revelations are not correctly understood. If we crave prophecies which are so clear and definite that they take from us the burden of responsible decision and loving abandonment to God's

83

inscrutable Providence, then what we want is sooth-saying and we are no longer capable of interpreting true prophecy aright should such emerge from a real 'apparition'.

Where private revelations (for example of new devotions) are taken as disclosing a spiritual trick, a method for acquiring holiness at little cost or changing the way of the Cross into pure joy; or where the entire spiritual life is reduced to revolving round one revelation (however genuine in itself), whose content, in comparison with the whole wide world of Christian truth by which we should live, is bound to be meagre — we can conclude that even genuine revelations have certainly been misunderstood and misapplied. On the other hand even the little gateway of a private revelation must be praised if by entering it people arrive at their first real grasp of Christianity, as often happens. Who would force these people of the little doors to enter God's house by the (really or supposedly) lofty portals of our great theology or of our own very private thought? On the other hand, however, one must not stop at the little door. Even the best devotion, which we should all practice, is not the whole of Christianity, and we are certainly not meant to conclude that it is if heaven recommends the devotion in a vision.

Though God speaks to us in divers ways, it is not clear *a priori* that his most important instructions will be given in visions. Rather they are contained in the Gospel and are proclaimed by the Church in its 'ordinary' preaching. God's Spirit stirs — sometimes, at least — even in the Church's theologians and various 'movements', even if they cannot appeal to visions. Lovers of revelations and apparitions should not forget either (as often happens) that Christ appears to us most surely in the poor and suffering. In the Sacrament and in the grace of the Holy Spirit, offered to every Christian, we have God's most real presence. The Cross is true mercy, and charity the highest of all gifts. If we do not recognize the hand that chastises us as God's merciful and healing hand, we shall not find him in 'revelations' either. The only good in any spirit is what makes us better Christians, and our conscience, trained by the spirit of the Church, tells pretty plainly what does that. This criterion will enable us to cope with real life, even though it may not settle the very theoretical question of whether a mental phenomenon comes directly or indirectly from the Spirit of God. What is left of visions and revelations after this test may still contain much that is human mingled with the divine, and it will be very difficult to distinguish the one from the other. A., therefore, must not force B. to see the divine in this particular human element, and B. must not dispute A.'s ability to find the divine in this same human element. The Church has always adopted this attitude and it will continue to do so.

In our own day, as always, the Church has gone about its duty to try the spirits with the utmost caution and sobriety. To my knowledge only three of the many apparitions of recent decades have been recognized: Fátima, Banneaux and Beauraing (both these latter places in Belgium having had apparitions in the years 1932 and 1933). Numerous other apparitions have either been actually condemned by episcopal authority or by the Holy Office, or else the Church has remained reserved, awaiting events and dissuading the faithful from accepting them. As evidence of the Church's caution in these matters we shall enumerate a few scenes of alleged apparitions during recent years which it has either condemned or refrained from approving. In alphabetical order they are: Acquaviva Platani (Sicily), Aspand (Lower Austria), Assisi (Italy), Bouxières-aux-Dames (France), La Codesera (Spain), Elz bei Limburg (Germany), Espis (France), Ezquioga (Spain), Forstweiler bei Tannhausen (Germany), Ghiaie di Bonate (Italy), Gimigliano (Italy), Hasznos (Hungary), Heede (Germany), Heroldsbach (Germany), Hintermailingen bei Lahr

(Germany), Hoesbach bei Aschaffenburg (Germany), Kayl (Luxembourg), Klausenburg (Transylvania), Le Bouchard (France), Liart (Belgium), Limpias (Spain), Lipa (Philippines), Lomnitz (Silesia), Petersberg-Rotalben (Germany), Pfaffenhofen a. d. R. (Germany), Lublin (Poland), Tre Fontane near Rome, Urucaina (Brazil).

This list could be considerably extended. It is noteworthy that these condemned apparitions often drew huge crowds (in Lublin in 1949, for instance, the weeping Madonna is said to have been visited by 100,000 people in one day; in 1939 70,000 people gathered on Mount Ezquioga in the Basque country) and that even the opposition of the faithful and of some clerics was unable to deflect ecclesiastical authority from its judgment (for instance at Heroldsbach and Bouxières-aux-Dames); that certain apparently miraculous answers to prayer on the occasion of pilgrimages etc., inspired by such apparitions, were not uncritically accepted by the Church authorities as divine confirmation of those visions (e.g. Ghiaie di Bonate), and that many such 'apparitions' strongly impress one as doubles of prior apparitions in other places (a series of appearances, a 'sun miracle', etc.). It is also evident that even today we are not necessarily secure against attempted fraud: the 'revelations' of Maria Rafols (d. 1853) which have been published since 1926 are a modern forgery; the 'apparitions' at Lipa in the Philippines were deliberately staged as a hoax; the visions at Gimigliano were invented by the little visionary after seeing the film on Bernadette (though many people claim to have seen the sun-miracle during those 'visions').

PART IV
Prophecies

Prophecies, insofar as they concern the religious sphere and claim divine origin, almost always occur as communications delivered by persons seen in visions, and thus claim supernatural origin in the same way as the apparitions themselves. The prophecies of La Salette[1] and of Catherine Emmerick, the predictions and promises of Fátima are examples. All that

---

[1] Cf. W. Widler, *Buch der Weissagungen* (8th ed., Munich, 1950), pp. 117 −128. More bibliography in *LThK* IX (1st. ed., 1937), col. 118 f. We must realize that the Church, and more specifically the Holy See, has repeatedly forbidden the propagation of the prophecies of La Salette. First, by two letters of Cardinal Caterini immediately after their publication by the visionary in 1879 (with the imprimatur of her spiritual director, the Bishop of Lecce). Then formally in 1901 and 1907 on the occasion of the condemnation of two books by Gilbert Combe on the secret of La Salette (*ASS* xxxiii [1900−1901], p. 677; xl [1907], p. 271). The most explicit and severe prohibition was issued in 1915. By this decree anyone who presumes to write about this secret in any manner whatsoever is threatened with the gravest penalties (*AAS* vii [1915], p. 594). Nevertheless, another book on the secret by H. Mariayè had to be condemned in the following year (*ASS* viii [1916] p. 178). A new edition of the secret was prohibited in 1923 (*AAS* xv [1923], pp. 287 f.). All this did not prevent Léon Bloy publishing the secret again in his book *Celle qui pleure*. He maintained that its first publication in 1872 had been blessed by Pius IX, while the edition of 1873 had received the approval of Cardinal Xyste-Riario Sforza. W. Widler holds his peace about all this (cf. Staehlin, *op. cit.,* p. 363 f. and note 29). More about La Salette in E. W. Roetheli, *La Salette. Das Buch der Erscheinung* (Olten, 1945), especially pp. 306, 308 ff.

has been said about the possibility and psychology of such apparitions in general, about the criteria of their authenticity and the compenetration of divine and human elements in them, will also apply to the prophecies given in these apparitions. Nevertheless, it will be useful to add a few separate remarks in their regard.

What we today call prophecy, that is a prediction or a foresight of a future event which could not be known by ordinary human means, occurs in the most various forms. Therefore it is difficult even to produce a typology of such prophecies. Yet we must not neglect the effort here since nothing intelligible can be said of prophecies unless their various types have been at least in some degree distinguished. Otherwise one would risk predicating the same things of, and giving the same criteria for, totally different phenomena. If we distinguish certain types of prophecies, of course it is done with the reservation that in concrete reality they may not occur as 'pure' types. Who, for instance, could exclude from the outset the possibility that in Catherine Emmerick's or Don Bosco's visions of the future[1] divine inspiration may have been combined with natural parapsychological forces? At any rate, in such cases, the supposition is not wholly impossible.

In the *first* type of prophecy I would classify all those phenomena which are best most clearly described as soothsaying, or divination in the pejorative sense of the term. In spite of the great differences there may be among them, I include here: oracular practices of classical and Germanic antiquity, astrology (insofar as it claims to be able to foretell details which depend on future free human decision),

---

[1] In the case of Don Bosco (as in that of C. Emmerick) the early occurrence of such phenomena (visions in dreams) seems rather to indicate a parapsychological inclination.

chiromancy or palmistry (insofar as it makes the same claim), fortune-telling from cards, soothsaying by questioning 'spirits' at seanaces, necromancy (conjuration of the dead in order to penetrate the future), etc. These things, while very different from each other, all fall into the category of superstition.

Superstitions they are, not only in the sense that the means are not proportionate to the end, and thus such practice is based on error and leads to illusions, but also because these practices spring from the soil of an irreligious attitude and in many cases may even imply readiness to entertain diabolic influences and activities, and to make use of these. Such practices leave the door wide open to delusion. Simply from the point of view of mental health all these things should be avoided as highly detrimental to people who indulge in them. The results of such practices, the prophecies arising from them, are practically always infantile and primitive — befitting the intellectual and moral standards of their adepts — which of itself suffices to show that they reveal no source of 'higher' knowledge. When, for instance, have the spirits at a seance ever said anything which was not as foolish and insignificant as the ideas and fancies already in the heads of the people who organized the occasion? Such superstitious divination is fundamentally irreligious, because on the one hand it is 'magical', that is, it claims to possess a technique for wresting God's secrets from him, and on the other hand because it dispenses altogether with the essential foundation of true religion, man's humble devotion to the sovereignty of the living God, whose ways and counsels are inscrutable; and it is in this devotion, and not in any knowledge of the future, that man finds true peace of heart. The main characteristic of such superstitious divination being an 'irreligious profanity', one could say conversely that where prophecy is irreligious (in the attitude from which it arises, in the belief that one has a sure technique for prophecy that can always be applied, etc.)

and profane (that is, at the service of worldly ambitions, of financial and similar advantages), the case is one of divination and must be rejected.

The *second* type of prophecy is of the 'parapsychological' kind, prophetic dreams, second sight, clairvoyance, foreknowledge of the hour of death, etc. Whether genuine phenomena of this nature exist is not an easy question to answer. Even if many instances are explained as illusions or interpreted in terms of normal psychology, a residue of such phenomena can neither be frauds nor coincidences, nor yet can they be explained by ordinary psychology. They may be called 'parapsychological', because though extraordinary they do not imply a special intervention of God but derive from natural faculties, even if these faculties are not — at least to any perceptible degree — at the disposal of the modern man of today. Supposing that one does not completely reject the reality of such phenomena, they must be attributed to natural powers, even if these be of an extraordinary character. For on the whole the achievements of these powers are from the religious point of view too insignificant to suggest a truly supernatural intervention of God. This does not mean, however, that they may not occur at times even in religious and saintly people, and that in them they may not serve some religious purpose. They seem often to be hereditary and endemic, associated with a certain region. If we call these prophecies 'parapsychological' it is only to assert their reality (or at least admit their possibility) and to distinguish them, as natural phenomena, form prophecies of divine origin. We are far from intending to explain these phenomena. Minds great and small have tried again and again, in the course of history, to explain how such visions of the future, of themselves natural, can come about. If one wished to write a history of these attempts, the names of Aristotle, St. Augustine, St. Thomas Aquinas, Leibniz, Jung-Stilling, Schopenhauer, E.

von Hartmann, Driesch, Willi Mooch and many others would have to be mentioned. However, it could not be said that all these attempts have shed much light on the question. For it is difficult indeed to explain how anybody could so rise above time as to encounter the future as if it were already present, if one is not to embrace an absolute determinism according to which the whole future, even free personal activity, is already fixed in present reality and therefore can be ascertained from the present.

However desirable it might be for us to know how such a vision of the future occurs, for my purpose — which is to distinguish parapsychological prophecies from those of divine origin — this is not absolutely necessary. We can draw an approximate distinction between them, even failing a full explanation. Where, for the reasons already mentioned, we have to assume a case of natural parapsychological clarvoyance, these phenomena exhibit characteristics by which they can be clearly distinguished (at least in general; we admit that there are difficult borderline cases) from prophecies of divine origin, of which we have examples in the Bible. The former are distinguished from the latter, not only by their content (the absence of any real religious purpose and of integration into a theological interpretation of history), but also psychologically. The parapsychological vision of the future is just a vision. That is, it shows a small, random part of the future, like an incidental cut from a long film, without reference to any larger, coherent event, without any interpretation, any accompanying person to impart the revelation and personally address the visionary. The parapsychological seer in some impersonal way seizes a shred of the future, which by some 'accident' is blown senselessly and blindly into the range of his observation. Whatever is seen is very clear and concrete, as if one were really there; the visionary can describe it like a reporter. But what is seen so clearly is isolated, and thus in

93

spite of all attempts at interpretation remains unintelligible. A divine prophecy is different. When the Lord of the world and history, transcendent over time, imparts information about the future, this is not a 'vision' (at least essentially) but a 'word'. It does not show a picture of part of the future, but communicates something about it together with an interpretation. In its details, therefore (because, not although, it comes from God), this communication will be obscure, because it speaks rather of the meaning of the future and does not wish to be a means by which one could protect oneself from it, but wishes to leave the future obscure so as to preserve man's freedom in valourous reliance on God. Its style, consequently, is not that of a reporter miraculously transported into the future, who then narrates what he experiences on the spot. Rather it will give the man to whom it is addressed the forward look into the future which he needs in order to endure his own present now with loyal confidence in God. In short: the first *is* a vision; the second is a word; the first is an anticipation of the future as if it were present; the second an anticipation of the future which remains a future.

In an individual case it will not always be easy to diagnose a prophecy as one type or the other through this general description of parapsychological and divine prophecy, the more so as an intermingling of these two types of phenomena cannot be excluded *a priori*. Still if we think, for example, of the prophecy of Muehlhiasl or that of the youth of Elz (assuming that both were true), we will see the position at once. Such predictions as these latter include some elements that are remarkably clear and some, at the same time, that are unintelligible; something is seen that is incomprehensible even for the seer himself. He does not know how far the vision reaches, whether it is a purely local event that may be totally unimportant for the history of the world, or whether it is the heart of future history. A religious interpretation, a theological and historical context for the vision, will at most be added by the seer on the basis of his other opinions and beliefs but is no part of the vision itself. Otherwise it would have to be given in the 'word', not in a vision, because a word, a concept, can comprehend the abstract, can condense and interpret the future; which a vision of the future as it really happens could not do unless (and this is impossible for other reasons) it were to present the whole long film of the future or a great part of it. And therefore it is safe to consider such prophecies as these parapsychological, natural and not supernatural.

For where God reveals himself with his knowledge of the future by a miraculous intervention, a religious purpose and interpretation are an intrinsic element of the communication about the future and God always speaks personally to the seer. Otherwise God would not be working a miracle contrary to the laws of nature. This is the only intelligible purpose of a miraculous divine communication and automatically explains the content and psychological characteristics of a divine prophecy. Where these are not verified all visions of the future (however 'true' in some sense) must be pronounced parapsychological phenomena, although we do not have as yet any precise and convincing theory of how they occur.

A *third* type anticipates the future (at least attempts to do so) in the light of the philosophy and theology of history. Great human minds have always looked to the future, sensed coming events, warned their contemporaries of the future consequences of the deeds of the present, consoled those who in their present had to sow in tears with the thought of the joyful harvest that coming generations would gather. Perhaps we should associate with this type the 'national prophecy' which 'accompanies the history of all peoples who have awakened to national consciousness' (J. Bernhart). Men like

St. Augustine, Nicholas of Cusa, Savonarola, Rousseau, Heine, Donoso Cortés, Soloviev, Nietzsche and others come to mind. However diverse their opinions and presuppositions, and consequently their anticipatory interpretations of history, these and similar 'prophets' all had frequent and uncannily accurate intuitions of the future, inseparable indeed from their particular historical perspective and limited accordingly. Obviously a variety of causes will conspire to produce 'prophecies' of this kind: the philosophical and historical perspicacity of a great mind, guidance from Scriptural prophecy and its theology of history, occasional parapsychological influences and perhaps even property supernatural ones. Generally speaking, however, predictions of the sort will bear the hallmark of their principal cause: the insight of human genius into historical developments already in embryo which will mould the more or less distant future. Therefore they will be a mixture of truth and falsehood, light and darkness; there will be partiality, oversights, misinterpretations. Many things will happen not because they were forseen, but because they were 'predicted' of a future 'utopia', which will attract people as a new ideal and inspire them to realize it. Here the future is not foretold because it is going to happen, it happens because it has been foretold. The 'prophet' does not foresee the future, but sets the men of the present a new goal — sometimes even by warning against it. "Talk of the devil and he is sure to appear", (as good Christians of our day who like to assume the mantle of Jeremiah and talk of impending doom should remember). As such prophecies always prove to be deduction from any analysis of the present, they can be distinguished from supernatural prophecy with relative ease. They are worth as much as the evidence on which they rest, that is, the analysis of thé present (correct or incorrect, balanced or unbalanced).

I shall briefly mention a *fourth* type: fabricated prophecies.

I mean not simply those crude illusions and frauds which constantly recur in all the forms of superstitious investigation of the future already classified as the first type of prophecy. Rather I have in mind examples such as the prophecies concerning future popes which are ascribed to St Malachy, or the 'prophecies of Lehnin' (a Cistercian monastery in Brandenburg), or those of St Ottilia. There is always a tendentious political or religious composition (often profoundly clever), which in the garb of prophecy propagates ideas on civil or ecclesiastical government and in some cases pronounces judgment on the past (which is presented as still in the future). I need say nothing more of fabricated prophecies, often as they have been believed and have swayed the thoughts and aspiration of men.

The *fifth* and last type of prophecy are genuine supernatural revelations of which God himself is the immediate cause. We shall have to discuss their real significance. A Christian who seriously believes the testimony of Scripture cannot doubt that such revelations are possible. Together with miracles they are the evidence in sacred history by which God confirms his message to humanity, given through the prophets and apostles, and manifests its divine origin. The Church teaches that they are motives of credibility.

The possibility of God's predicting the future is quite consistent with the Christian concept of God, difficult as it may be to see precisely how God can know the future without prejudice to its 'futurity' and especially to its freedome. As the living and omniscient God he transcends time and history. As the omnipotent First Cause sustaining all creation, that is, all reality other than himself, he is equally close to everything that happens or is to happen in time. Time is an intrinsic modality of all 'becoming' in creation but not a modality of God's relationship to the world. Therefore the future is not such for God himself. For God the future is the present.

Therefore he can make it known if he wishes to do so.

We would not maintain that this classification is absolutely complete, nor that it is always easy to assign a concrete prophecy to one of our five types. One might ask, for instance, whether diabolic prophecies are possible or actuall exist, a question which must engrossed the Fathers of the Church. Again one might ask how we should classify the famous prophecy of Nostradamus. But I shall not pursue these matters here.

We shall now endeavour to say something about the theology of prophecy.

Divination, in the sense I have defined, is morally wrong. It is either an attempt to achieve an end by using inappropriate means, or it is an explicit or implicit attempt to invoke diabolic powers. Both are morally wrong. Here the Christian must still say: 'There is no soothsaying in Jacob, nor divination in Israel' (Num. 23:23). (Cf. Lev. 19:26 and 31; Deut. 18:9—14.) According to Canon Law the bishop must combat and punish 'superstition' (*CIC* can. 2325), and this is doubtless particularly applicable to divination. Catholics may not take part in spiritualist conversations and manifestations (Decree of Holy Office, April 24, 1917; *Denz.* 2182). Thus the Church forbids seances whereever, and insofar as, such parapsychological phenomena (real or supposed) are sought and are evoked in the hope of communications from the other world (from the dead, or 'spirits', etc.), wherever these natural parapsychological phenomena are not investigated out of serious scientific interest and on the basis of an 'animistic' theory, with proper scientific sobriety, but people do those things because they are supposed to elicit information from the spiritual world. This will be true especially where such spiritualistic practices are developed into a system 'Occultism', etc. Decree of the Holy Office, July 18, 1919; *Denz.* 2189). The scriptural account of a very early case of necromancy with the object of learning about the future (1 Kings 28:5—25) is still worth reading. Such 'spirits' even today might well ask the participant in a spiritualist seance: 'Why askest thou me, seeing the Lord has departed from thee, and is gone over to thy rival?' But where one is convinced that the results of such spiritualistic seances actually come from the subconscious of the participants, which is usually the case, the possibility of obtaining any information about the future is automatically excluded.

As to visions of the future which are really parapsychological (that is natural, though extraordinary, mental phenomena — if and so far as they exist) there is nothing more to be said from the religious and theological point of view. They occur involuntarily, and therefore the seer can have no moral responsibility for them, the less so as they seldom or never enable him to act differently in view of such knowledge than he would have done without it. As there is no really reliable method of causing these natural visions of the future, I need not broach the question of how to behave if there were.

I have already stated how the foresights of great minds resulting from their studies of the philosophy and theology of history are to be theologically evaluated: they are worth as much as the arguments which those men adduce in their support from a rational or intuitive analysis of the present. If they invoke the revealed principles of the theology of history, or interpret a prophecy contained in revelation, it is necessary to ascetain whether these deductions and interpretations are correct, and whether they can be understood literally of the near future (which is not usually the case). Prophecies of the historical future which modern sects (Jehovah's Witnesses, Adventists, etc.) think they find in the Apocalypse of St John are based entirely on an arbitrary misinterpretation of biblical revelation. The doctrine that Christ will visibly reign on earth for a thousand years before the last judgment and the consummation of all things has been repeatedly condemned by the Church in very recent times as a misinterpreation of the Apocalypse (Reply of the Holy Office, July 11, 1941; *Denz.* 2296).

Finally a word should be said on correctly understanding real God-given revelations of the future. Scripture testifies that genuine divine prophecy is possible and has in fact occurred. Suffice it to recall Christ's prediction of the destruction of Jerusalem. To deny the possibility of such predictions in principle would therefore offend against the Catholic faith. Prophecy is also to be a permanent endowment of the Church and a proof of its supernatural mission. Therefore the prophetic genius will never die out in the Church. There will always be men in the Church with charismatic gifts, who will look into the future like the prophets of old and warn us to make the right decisions in the present. This is not to say that all the prophecies, even of saints, must be authentic and accurace. A few examples have been cited above to show that even saints have been deceived in their visions of the future. An absolute criterion of a genuine-prophecy can be found, before its fulfilment, only in what we have shown to be the sole proof of a genuine vision (for others than the seer): namely a miracle (of a different sort) which is demonstrated to be such, and is performed in such connection with the prophecy that it can really be taken as its divine confirmation. The truth of a prophecy is not confirmed, for instance, if miracles occur during a pilgrimage to the scene of a vision, but not in such connection with the prophecy as to be regarded as its divine confirmation,[1] or if

---

[1] A distinction is therefore made between miracles of confirmation and miracles of mercy. The latter are granted by God in view of and as a reward for the great faith and confidence with which a person approaches him seeking help. They are, however, not given as a confirmation of visions which previously occurred at the place in question. Cf. J.

such a connection cannot be proved beyond all doubt. Even if one assumes the sun-miracle of Fátima to be a true miracle, it would not prove that the seer's revelation of the future have received the divine seal. The miracle occurs to confirm the vision,[2] but it does not follow that every pronouncement of the visionary on the future is warranted, especially since this information about the future was only disclosed at a

Lhermitte, *Le problème des miracles* (Paris, 1956), pp. 57–71. The author refers here to a miracle granted at Port Royal to a niece of Blaise Pascal during the time when the nuns were in rebellion against the ecclesiastical authorities.

[2] It might be interesting to give here a brief summary of the revelations (disclosures and prophecies) of Fátima which became known before 1935 and 1941 (or more precisely, before 1927, in which year Canon Formigao's book was published). Concerning the first apparition: When Lucia asked on May 13th about the whereabouts of two girls who had recently died, the apparition answered that one of them was in heaven and the other in purgatory (L. G. da Fonseca, *Mari spricht zur Welt* [1952] p, 21). On September 27 Lucia said it had been revealed to her that St. Joseph would appear with the chold Jesus on October 13 and give the world peace and that the Mother of God would work a miracle on that day (this latter only when Lucia asked what Our Lady intended to do so that people should believe Lucia) (Visconde de Montelo, *op. cit.*, p. 76). On the evening of October 13, Lucia said 'She said that we should become better, that we should not insult our Lord, because he has already been insulted so much; that we should say the rosary and beg for the remission of our sins, that the war will end *today* and that we should expect our soldiers to return very soon' (*idib.*, 99). This statement was confirmed on the 19th: 'She said: 'The war will end this very day, and people here should expect their returning soldiers very soon'. And: 'I said it (on October 13) exactly as Our Lady said it' (*idib.*, p. 109) On the same 19th of October Lucia also said that the apparition revealed to her on August 19, or on the 13th of some month, that Christ would appear on October 13 in order to bless the world, and Our Lady of Sorrows as well (*idib.*, p. 113). On November 2 Jacinta finally said that the apparition had revealed on August 19 that if the children had not been taken to Ourem on the 13th St. Joseph would have come with the child Jesus to bring peace to the world (*idib.*, p. 121).

much later date.[1] Such reservations are even more appropriate in the case of the prophecies which allegedly derive from the visionaries of La Salette.[2]

As to the purpose of such divine prophecies, we must first state that they cannot be intended to restrict human liberty. Being divine interventions whose purpose is human salvation, they will not take from man the burden and grace of free

[1] In 1941. The books on Fátima published before that date know nothing about them. We mean the following predictions: Jesus wishes to establish devotion to the Immaculate Heart of Mary through Lucia (*Maria spricht zur Welt*, pp. 31 f., 42). Not long after the present was (1914-1918) another war will break out during the pontificate of Pius IX unless people amend their lives. An unknown light will be the sign announcing it. Them the 'request that Russia be consecrated to the Immaculate Heart; if this is done Russia will be converted; if not, Russia will spread her errors and the good will suffer martyrdom. In the end will come the triumph of the Immaculate Heart and the conversion of Russia, which will be consecrated to it by the Holy Father. Several nations will be annihilated' (*idib.*, p. 42 f.). When asked in 1946: 'Is it not a pity that the secret was not revealed before the war?' — Lucia answered: 'Well, if God had wanted to present me to the whole world as a prophetess then it really would have been a pity. But it seems that was not his intention . . .' (*idib.*, p. 291; the three dots are also there). But how is it comprehensible that God should *reveal* certain matters concerning the whole world to a person, in order that this person should keep them *secret* until after their fulfilment? Or what can we say of a mission to establish a certain devotion (one should rather say, to promote a devotion, the devotion to the Immaculate Heart of Mary has been known for over a hundred years) if this mission was given as a secret with a strict order for it to be strictly guarded? Even if it be said that the time for secrecy has now run out, we still are faced with a unique instance of God giving an order twenty-five years before he wishes it carried out.

[2] It is a remarkable coincidence that Mélanie made her first attempt to publish the secret — she left the Carmelite convent in Darlington for this purpose — in 1858, the year in which the apparitions occurred at Lourdes and attracted attention (cf. L. Bloy, *Celle qui pleure*, p. 112 f.).

decision in courageous and trusting faith. They do not intend to provide man with a device for cleverly avoiding the difficult passages of history and securing himself a safe and comfortable life (from the worldly point of view). They are not instructions for fleeing the cross of Christ. Where prophecies are so understood they are misunderstood, though genuine and of divine origin in themselves. Divine prophecy has a different sense and object; it is to manifest the living God as the Lord of history, even the history of darkness. Such prophecy would tell us that the seemingly hopeless situations of the world and the kingdom of Christ in it, do not mean that God has lost control of history, but were taken into account in the plans of his Providence from the beginning, because he wishes to triumph through our weakness. Divine prophecies will warn us against wordly optimism, against the mania for progress and against the utopian attempt to realize on this earth a kingdom of universal bliss. For this reason they constantly announce a dark future. True prophecies call us to penance, conversion, prayer, trust in the victory of Christ, hope in God eternal. Post-apostolic prophecies must fit into the framework of scriptural prophecy if they would be acknowledged as genuine. Consequently they will tell us nothing essentially new beyond the scriptural perspective and interpretation of the future; but at the same time they will be concrete and timely imperatives for our day, deriving from the general theology of the future and of history which Scripture already gives us. Their real sense will be an imperative for the right attitude towards a future which always remains dark and threatening, which is always forfeit to death (from a wordly point of view) and yet is profitable for the salvation of those who believe and love.

Prophecy, according to 1 Corinthians 13:9, is a mere fragment in comparison to charity, which alone has the strength to embrace even the perpetual darkness of the future, which no prophecy could so illumine as to banish all dangers from it. For love alone can accept such a future from the hands of God as a gift of his wisdom and his love. There will ever be true and false prophets in the kingdom of Christ (Matt. 10:41). So the exhortation is always opportune, 'extinguish not the spirit; despise not prophecies; but prove all things; hold fast that which is good' (1 Thess. 5:19-21). The good in every prophecy is ultimately shown if it awakens us to the gravity of decision in courageous faith, if it makes clear to us that the world is in a deplorable state (which we never like to admit), if it steels our patience and fortifies our faith that God has already triumphed, even if in this world we still have distress, if it fills us with confidence in the one Lord of the still secret future, if it brings us to prayer, to conversion of heart, and to faith that nothing shall separate us from the love of Christ.

Date Due

Demco 38
